DELIVERANCE

THE MACMILLAN COMPANY
NEW YORK · BOSTON · CHICAGO · DALLAS
ATLANTA · SAN FRANCISCO

MACMILLAN & CO., Limited
LONDON · BOMBAY · CALCUTTA
MELBOURNE

THE MACMILLAN CO. OF CANADA, Ltd.
TORONTO

DELIVERANCE

THE FREEING OF THE SPIRIT IN THE ANCIENT WORLD

BY

HENRY OSBORN TAYLOR, Litt.D.

New York

THE MACMILLAN COMPANY

1915

Norwood Press
J. S. Cushing Co. — Berwick & Smith Co.
Norwood, Mass., U.S.A.

IN MEMORIAM

SAMUEL ISHAM

CONTENTS

DELIVERANCE

PROLOGUE

WE have Homer's word for it, that not all dreams are from Zeus. No truly! Dreams are as foolish as the gibbering of souls in Orcus — till they, souls or dreams, have drunk the blood of waking. But a wise country lies before the gates of sleep, and vistas of insight come to them who are waiting there. Very different from dreams, these wakeful watches of the night, when thought, disentangled from the day's variety, is spontaneous and limpid.

Recently with me such waking hours have been made peaceful by thought of freedom from anxiety over the ways of men, even by thought of that final peace or freed activity, which is death. But however fruitful or fruitless these "night thoughts," there surely follows the disturbing yet wholesome correction of the forenoon's intending of the mind. For be sure, O possible gentle reader, that I subject to the sober verification of the day whatever in the watches of the night came as happy intuition.

Often turning back through my scattered

knowledge of the past, I see that these thoughts of mine are old, and that they have done duty in the minds of men before me. One finds them harnessed in the systems of those Great Ones, those apparent sources of the world's convictions, who in their time set in new-found relationships, and made living, the *disjecta membra* of human experience and casual reflection. Yet the thoughts may be ours as well as theirs, by virtue of the very same title of having them flash joyfully upon the mind.

One realises a universal kinship in human need and aspiration when following such thoughts seemingly afar in the minds of these Founders who have passed on. They who may have died ages ago are nearer to us than the alien masses among whom we move. They are the spiritual fathers of us all, and we make ourselves consciously their sons by coming to know them in their achieved or striven for adjustment of themselves with the eternal, and in their attunement of their desires to human limitations. Some men live in the eternities, and must at their peril keep in tune with them. The need of adjustment belongs to them peculiarly. Yet, in some degree, it pertains to all who are touched with meditation; and the endeavour for it, which is an endeavour for peace and spiritual freedom, is an element of life which carries across centuries

and millenniums. Although that which those
Ancients reached, or even that which they tried for,
may not be for us, still the contemplation of their
efforts is as the effect of noble sculpture and
poetry, bringing something like the final calm,
the emotional purge, of tragedy.

In some such way my thoughts set themselves
in the watches of the night, and were confirmed or
criticised in the hours of the day. They have
encouraged me to attempt some ordering and
statement of the ways in which our spiritual
ancestors of all times and countries adjusted themselves to the fears and hopes of their natures, thus
reaching a freedom of action in which they accomplished their lives; or, it may be, they did
but find peace; yet brought it forth from such
depth of conviction that their peace became peace
for thousands and for millions. It did not seem
well to enter circumstantially upon the antecedents or even the setting of these men, for fear
these "watches of the night" might become a
history of human conviction. Nor will the at-
tention be more than casually directed to the
ways in which they were influenced, or influenced
others. I would set forth rather in themselves,
and simply, those individuals who most clearly
illustrate phases of human adjustment with life, its
limitations, aspirations, and conceived determining
powers, working within or from without.

But however we may seek to simplify our reflections, we cannot limit ourselves to any one category of adjustment. The needs of men are not the same universally; and the human adjustment may relate to conduct or to speculation, to distress at life's chain of torment, or to fear of extinction; it may relate to the impulse to speculate and know, or to the need to be "saved." For one man shall find his peace in action, another in the rejection of action, even in the seeming destruction of desires. Another shall have peace and freedom through intellectual enquiry, while another must obey his God, or love his God, and may stand in very conscious need of divine salvation. The adjustment sought by Confucius was very different from that which drew the mind of Plato, or led Augustine to the City of God. Often quite different motives may inspire the reasonings which incidentally bring men to like conclusions. The Absolute Brahma of the Upanishads and the Being of Parmenides have certain common metaphysical foundations; but the motives impelling the Hindu and the Eleatic to somewhat similar results were as different as the Greek and Indian temperaments, — as different as those which likewise brought Gotama and Heracleitus to the conviction that existence is ceaseless flux. The life-adjustment of the early Greek philosophers had to do with scientific curiosity; they were seeking hypothetical explanations of the world about them, themselves perhaps implicitly included; they were not, like Gotama, seeking relief from the tedious impermanence of personal experience, any more than they were seeking to assure their own eternal welfare in and through the love of God — the motive around which surged the Christian yearning for salvation. Evidently every "religion" is a means of adjustment, or deliverance; but there are other adjustments, which are not religious in any current acceptation of the word.

There is an advantage in commencing, and it may be ending, with the seers of the ancient world, and their early Christian successors to the suffrages of men. For they are fundamental, verily elemental in their exemplifications of the main divisions of the human need for an adjustment between the instincts and faculties of human nature and the powers conceivably controlling its accomplishment and destiny. We shall never altogether issue from between the projected lines of their achievement, however far we may seem to have advanced.

CHAPTER I

CHALDÆA AND EGYPT

WHEN did the need for adjustment begin?
To answer this is to answer the unanswerable
question — when did men begin? Thirty thousand
years ago, on the cave walls at Altamira, there
were paintings of animals, possibly carrying tote-
mistic import. Without disturbing these "pre-
historic" enigmas, we may more fruitfully consider
"historic" beginnings, say in Chaldæa and Egypt,
— these being ancient times for us, when men's
so-called minds were filled with notions which
human experience has since found irrational and
indeed incomprehensible.

It is always difficult for one time to understand
another; among contemporaries mutual understanding rarely extends beyond the range of congeniality! With physical needs fundamentally the
same, men have always been desirous, restless,
apprehensive, anticipating evils real or imaginary,
striving to guard against them, — evils of this life
or touching existence after death. Although archaic
adjustments with imagined anxieties seem so foolish
now, the underlying human nature and human need
are related to ourselves. Hundreds of thousands

6

of men and women are seeking to adjust themselves
with the eternal ways, and hope to see the everlasting stars. All is mystery still, albeit the forces
holding man are no longer "supernatural," and the
desired adjustment refers little to the life to come.
Let no one think that he has shaken off the past!
We are in and of it, if we are also of ourselves.
Our thoughts and the images in which we clothe
them, what ancestry they trail out of a dim and
ever lengthening distance, back through Rome to
Greece, and through Greece backward still and
eastward to the valleys of the Nile and the Eu-
phrates. And there the receding trail only begins,
for further back it passes, not ceasing, only to our
blindness vanishing in a remote and semihuman
past.

It is well to recognise the pit from which we have
been digged. Therefore, if for no other purpose,
let us contemplate, for a little, one or two ancient
lines of attempted adjustment, of endeavour after
some sort of spiritual deliverance, to which the name
of no individual attaches, but rather that of a
people or a land, in this case Mesopotamia and
Egypt. The peoples of Mesopotamia as well as
the Egyptians accumulated a colossal material
equipment, and made a large advance in the social
ordering of life. A certain King Hammurapi has
of late years become the central figure of Meso-
potamian history. At the opening of the second

millennium before Christ, he established the Kingdom of Babylon, and reigned as a King of law and
righteousness, as well as might.   It was a period,
it was indeed a land, of trade and agriculture, regu-
lated by law and custom.   Hammurapi issued a
code of laws, the most signal legal document of far
antiquity, and a worthy predecessor for the civil
law of Rome, of which it may have been a remote
and partial source.   Thus the Babylonian people
show how deftly they had settled themselves in
their human relationships, and had reached some
facile freedom of conduct.   Yet their lives were
overhung with dread.   They were very fearful of
the unseen — of the imagined powers which they
sought to coerce by magic, or move through prayer.
They had thus devised nostrums for their hampering fears, and yet had found no sure stay for their
furthest hopes — dreary at best, and at worst filled
with horror, was existence within and beyond the
grave.   No spell or prayer had been devised to
help the dead.   Magic and prayer, the warning of
the sheep's liver, the portents of the storm, the phases
of sun and moon and stars, availed only the living.

As the centuries went on, the Babylonians and
Assyrians improved their conceptions of the Gods;
ascribed justice to them, beneficence, righteousness,
even pity.   Yet always with fear and abasement:
"Thy slave who bears the weight of thy wrath
is covered with dust"; and centuries later Nebu-

chadnezzar says that he *loves* the fear of God. There had also come to the Babylonians and Assyrians quite positive thoughts of their own shortcomings, omissions, social crimes. All such delinquencies, when thought of with reference to the gods, fell within the category of *sin*. They bewailed their sins prostrate before their gods, and begged forgiveness. Yet they never distinguished clearly between involuntary oversight and intended wrong. Ceremonial omission, eating or treading on the forbidden thing, brought divine anger with plague and punishment, just as quickly as fraud, incest, and murder. There also rose among them the wailing cry of perplexity over the good man brought low, the cry of one who has done his best and yet has been afflicted : "If I only knew that such things were pleasing before God ! But that which seems good to a man is evil before God. Who may understand the counsel of the gods in heaven ?" [1]

At all events, for him who has been guilty, as for him who can find in himself no sin, penitence and abasement can only affect the remainder of his days on earth. After death the same fate awaits the evil and the good, and no help for either. Satisfaction, vengeance, sense-gratification, the pleasures of daily life and the tranquillising occupations of

[1] Zimmern, *Babylonische Hymnen*, etc., pp. 27, 29. Jastrow, "A Babylonian Parallel to Job," *Journal of Biblical Lit.*, Vol. XXV.

labour, — all were had in this rich river land; its material welfare and order, the degree of civilisation there attained, attest the existence of a sufficiency of practical justice and law-abidingness. But Mesopotamia never evolved either a religion, a philosophy, or an ethical scheme that could lead the human spirit to freedom or peace.

It may be doubted whether the Egyptians thought more clearly; but their temperament was different, and their lives would seem to have been calm and stable. All this, however, is no explanation of the marvels of constructive foolishness, no explanation whatsoever of the grossly impossible continuation of life after death, which they fabricated. It is natural as well as universal not to think of death as ending all; the natural man has neither the data nor a sufficient clarity of mind to reach the notion of extinction. His impulse is to imagine how the dead can go on under conditions so obviously changed. But any elaboration of such imaginings is apt to bear an inverse relation to his intelligence and power to discern inconsistencies. The Egyptian fabrication of a cumulative scheme of life beyond the tomb was unhampered by any sense of the impossible. Provision for it had to be made on earth, and the expense was beyond the means of all except Pharaohs and the great nobles. Pyramids bulwarked the post-mortem life of Egypt's kings. The texts within set forth the further means whereby that existence should be continued and supported, should be filled with authority, dignity, occupation, supplied with dainty food and with pleasures distinctly of the flesh. Every measure was taken to make the post-mortem life of Pharaoh and his nobles as luxurious as if they still commanded countless slaves on earth. Their tombs were furnished with symbolical conveniences, with serving statuettes, and chapters from the Book of the Dead, which magically caused these statuettes to do the work of men in the nether world. The venal sacerdotal imagination encompassed that subterranean life with dangers at every turn, and even devised conditions of sinfulness, so that priests and scribes might also furnish, for a price, charms to quell the dangers and scrolls to disavow the sinfulness, just as Indulgences pertaining to the nether world were to be bought for money three thousand years afterwards. Yet during those early Egyptian centuries, a clearer morality introduced rewards and punishments into the scheme of the life to come. To some extent, the post-mortem welfare of the great, and possibly of the lowly, became dependent on the virtues of their lives on earth.

In this combination of ethical thought with means magical, religious, or material, for supporting life beyond the tomb, lay the most striking Egyptian endeavour to free the human spirit from fear, and adjust man to the conditions and possibilities of his life. As a part of this freeing of the spirit, Egyptian conceptions of the divine gained ethical discrimination and universal breadth. The gods, or the one god for the moment deemed supreme, would be less capricious if clothed with right and justice, and could, if omnipotent, bear more efficient aid. A surer sense of peace was won, as men realised the might of the divine favour, and more clearly saw, or thought they saw, how it should be won and held. Their gods were righteous, and would save the righteous; and their power was adequate since they, or rather the momentarily supreme one among them, had come to be conceived as Lord and Creator not of Egypt alone, but of all earth's lands, and as supreme also in the world of the still sentient dead. The final intimate comfort came with the thought that this eternal Lord and Maker of Life might also enter the king's heart, and bring him wisdom and life. God had become the mother and father of all that he had made, and had filled Egypt with his love. One king at least, the revolutionary Amenhotep IV (C. 1375 B.C.), possessed these thoughts, and could pray that his eyes might be satisfied daily with beholding Aton (the supreme and universal Sun-god) when he dawns in his temple, and fills it with his own self by his beams, loving and life-giving forever.

The name was nothing. Aton had taken many of the qualities of Amon and Osiris; and when the name of Aton was stamped out in the succeeding reaction, Amon received back from his rival attributes which had once been his, but which in Aton had come to added grace and power. And then a last advance was made; these beautiful conceptions spread themselves among men, even among those of low estate, whose lot in by-gone times had been scant burial and scant equipment for any life thereafter. Amon had become a god coming to the silent, saving the poor, listening to the cry of their affliction. "O Amon-Re, I love thee and I have filled my heart with thee. Thou wilt rescue me out of the mouth of men in the day when they speak lies: for the Lord of Truth, he liveth in truth." [1]

[1] See Breasted, *Religion and Thought in Ancient Egypt,* pp. 334, 355 and *passim.*

CHAPTER II

CHINA: DUTY AND DETACHMENT

CHINESE meditation, quietism, individualistic inaction, as well as the more constructive social energies of the race, reached personal exemplification and classic expression at about the same time in two remarkable personalities. Lao Tzu and Confucius were Chinese incarnations of the *vita contemplativa* and the *vita activa*, the βίος θεωρητικός and πρακτικός. One might whimsically call them the Mary and Martha of China.

These two modes of human life may rest on different motives and assume different forms with different peoples. The contemplative life may issue from the detached intellectual temperament, which is supremely interested in knowing, or it may issue from brooding aversion to life's more blatant activities, or from horror over a sinful world and fearful or loving consecration to one's own salvation and the God with whom that lies. The active life may embrace many and diverse intellectual interests, may have religious or secular aims, may represent devotion to the social fabric or fierce ambition.

For the sake of clarity one distinguishes these

tendencies rather sharply, and speaks of them as opposites. But, of course, they mingle in the same individuals. Moreover, in every land, those who exhibit markedly one tendency will have much in common with those who represent the other, because of like environment and racial characteristics underlying the idiosyncrasies of individuals. So the views of Confucius and Lao Tzu show affinity as well as opposition. It is better to speak first of Confucius, because Lao Tzu, although the elder by some fifty years, embodies a reaction against the more dominant Chinese qualities represented in the younger man.[1]

How did Confucius consider life and his relationship to the world, and set himself to reach such freedom in thought and corresponding act as he was capable of ? He may seem a very bounden man ; but he was free, though his freedom lay in reverent self-adaptation to chains — as they appear to us. Confucius looked sadly upon the state of affairs about him, and with admiration on the past as he read it in that ancient history and poetry which he tended with such care. He wished to conform his conduct to the ways of ancient worthies, and raise the misrule of the Chinese princes to the measure of the (imagined) government of the ancient (imagined) kingdom. In the adjustment of his conduct, he appears to have been faultless ; and

[1] Confucius' birth is securely set at 551 B.C.

while he realised little of his public purpose, he did much to prescribe the ideal which China has ever since revered. His life began with learning, and continued learning many things, the wisdom of the ancient sages and the appointed rites and ceremonies. With this went ceaseless effort to perform the rites, and make them the garment of a character conforming to the Way of Heaven, whose sure and righteous power presented the ultimate sanction of conduct, — and so the standard of man's life-adjustment. It was all established in the narratives and teaching of the old History: "The way of Heaven is to bless the good, and make the bad miserable"; again, "It was not that Heaven had any private partiality for the lord of Shang; it simply gave its favour to pure virtue." And the old History also taught as an inspiration that "The glory and tranquillity of a state may arise from the goodness of one man." [1]

Accordingly, the entire endeavour of Confucius was to model his conduct upon the Way of Heaven as illustrated in the Book of History and the over-interpreted teaching of the classic Odes. By this means his character would become such that his life and precepts might tranquillise the land, a result which might be hoped for, as the Shu King said, from the goodness of one man.

[1] The closing words of the *Shu King* (the classic Book of History). Legge's Translation.

Says Confucius, speaking of the stages of his progress: "At fifteen my mind was bent on learning; at thirty I stood firm; at forty I had no doubts; at fifty I knew the decrees of Heaven; at seventy I could follow what my heart desired, without transgressing."[1] So through a long life came his adjustment, conforming to the most surely sanctioned standards that he could conceive, and bringing with it spiritual peace and freedom.

The contents of this adjustment will be seen to include an endless series of observances, minute, meticulous, painful, — the conventions, ceremonies, rites, controlling the intercourse of society, and prescribing the ceremonials of marriage, burial, ancestor worship, worship of Heaven, and propitiation of all the spirits affecting human lots for good or ill. These rules of propriety and rites and ceremonies illustrate the graded distinctions obtaining between Heaven and earth. To know them and carry them out reverently will mould the character aright. The finish comes from Music, which exhibits the Harmony prevailing between earth and Heaven.[2]

Thus music and ceremonies supplement each other, and unite in the Confucian scheme. Within, the character and will must correspond with the

[1] *Confucian Analects*, II, 4. Legge's Translation.
[2] See the great collection of the *Li Ki*, translated by Legge; *Sacred Books of the East*, Vols. 27 and 28.

truth and righteousness of the Way of Heaven. "The Superior Man in everything considers righteousness to be essential. He performs it according to the rules of propriety — bringing it forth in humility, completing it in sincerity." He seeks truth rather than emolument; and is distressed only at his own shortcomings, not at poverty, ill-treatment, or death. He seeks friendship with the upright, not with the glib-tongued; he finds enjoyment in the study of ceremonies and music, not in idleness and feasting; he guards himself against lust, anger, avarice; he stands in awe of the ordinances of Heaven, of great men, and of the words of the sages.

Certain disciples suspected that the Master was obsessed with the learning of many things. Perceiving this, he said: "Those who know virtue are few. I seek a unity all-pervading." It was asked what these words might mean, and the answer came from one of the disciples: "The doctrine of our Master is to be true to the principles of our nature and the benevolent exercise of them toward others."

The correlated unity of the whole matter is made to appear in the most comprehensive of Confucian statements: "What Heaven has conferred is called the Nature: an accordance with this Nature is called the Path; the regulation of the Path is called Instruction.

"The Path may not be left for an instant. If it

could be left, it would not be the Path. On this account the superior man does not wait till he sees things, to be cautious, nor till he hears things, to be apprehensive. . . .

"While there are no stirrings of pleasure, anger, sorrow, or joy, the mind may be said to be in the state of Equilibrium. When those feelings have been stirred, and they act in their due degree, there ensues what may be called the state of Harmony. This Equilibrium is the great root, and this Harmony is the universal Path.

"Let the states of Equilibrium and Harmony exist in perfection, and a happy order will prevail throughout heaven and earth, and all things will flourish." [1]

That is to say, these principles, properly filled out with the accumulated precepts of political and social wisdom, will, if observed, insure the tranquillity of the state and produce correct and reverent ties between ruler and people, father and son, husband and wife, elder brother and younger, and between friend and friend.

Here is presented, not altogether clearly, the standard and the sanction of Confucius' adjustment of his life to the order of Heaven — which is

---

[1] This is from Chapter I of the *Chung Yung*, or *Doctrine of the Mean*, ascribed to the grandson of Confucius, and recognised as an authoritative statement of the Master's teaching. Cf. also, *ib.*, II, 8.

the aggregate of the divine spontaneously creative forces and man's share of them which constitutes his nature. Conformity to Heaven's high ordainments — to the Path — frees the sage from the fear of all things opposed or irrelevant to these his rules of conduct. The people also should be kept in like free conformity; — they should be instructed in the rules of propriety and should be led through their virtue, not coerced by laws. "The Master said: 'If the people be led by laws, and uniformity be sought to be given them by punishments, they will try to avoid the punishment, but will have no sense of shame. If they be led by virtue, and uniformity be sought to be given them by the rules of propriety, they will have the sense of shame, and, moreover, will become good.'"

But there was need of exertion on the part of rulers to keep the people in the Path — that had been the way of the ancient sage Emperors. Virtuous and energetic ministers should be employed, and not the useless. Possibly, when all things were well administered, the ruler himself might gravely and sedately, without active exertion, occupy his throne.

One observes that this cautious Chinaman, in his adjustment, did not go beyond the necessary assurance of his convictions, and refused to discuss from the religious or metaphysical point of view the ordinances of Heaven, or death, or the service of the spirits of the dead. Such matters did not fall within the needs of his personal adjustment, nor within the needs of his mission to his land.

Turning now to Taoism, and observing what its doctrines had in common with the system of Confucius, one notices first the name. That was taken from the broad Confucian, or rather Chinese, conception of the *Tao*, — meaning the Path, the Way or Method. While retaining these meanings, Tao also drew to itself in the thought of Lao Tzu and Chuang Tzu (perhaps his greater follower) a complementary meaning, that of the universal power, to wit, "Heaven" or nature spontaneously creative — of which Tao is the Way. Likewise the Tao of man and beast might be not only the Way but also the Nature of man and beast. Then, through a suppression of distinctions or a union of contraries, Tao became an obscurely conceived Absolute. Neither Confucianism nor Taoism had any definite conception of a God above Nature and distinct from it; although both drew current notions of invisible spirit-existences or influences from the common fund of Chinese superstition and tradition. Both systems emphasized the effect of virtue and character, — the exertionless influence of the sage. But, besides this, Confucius taught the regular efficiency of action and exertion on the sage's part, while Lao Tzu insisted on despising it.

To Confucius the web of proprieties was nearly all in all; while Lao Tzu relied consistently on the inherent virtue of the Tao. Thus it was that the former held fast to the thought (so replete with the "proprieties") of *reciprocity:* Do not, of course, do ill to any man; but recompense goodness with goodness, and evil with justice, — the last thought may sanction punishment if not revenge. But Lao Tzu, holding fast to the goodness of the Tao, would treat evil with goodness, of a mild and passive sort, one may imagine; and would not take up the foolish way of exertion in order to punish the evil-doer. It fell in with Taoism to emphasise the passive virtues of gentleness and humility, approved likewise by Confucius. Beyond this, the inaction and indifference of Taoism proceeded easily along the lofty, somewhat scornful, path of the obliteration of differences and identification of opposites.

One may contemplate with advantage and amusement the manner of the life-adjustments of Lao Tzu, and Chuang Tzu, who stand to each other, only with more generations between, as Socrates to Plato. Lao Tzu, a deliciously enigmatic person, appears, if Taoist sources may be trusted, to have quite dumfounded Confucius in a most improbable interview; he left a composition since called the *Tao-te-King*, of which, however, his authorship has been strenuously denied. The work represents at all events the more amorphous strata of Taoist doctrine, and one may as well ascribe it to this incomprehensible dragon of a Lao Tzu. The trans-

lations vary; [1] and no man knows what Lao Tzu
meant by Tao. Doubtless he himself did not
know, a fact to comfort us and lead to better understanding on our part. Whatever we make of Tao,
the book represents an adjustment of an individual
to his world, with thoughts touching the fussiness
of men over the unimportant. It also is as a hall
of echoes, where one catches mocking notes of
Brahma, of Heracleitus, or of Jesus.

Lao Tzu, like Confucius, lived when China was a
group of disorderly and often hostile states. Past
and present were in his mind. Had there not been
in the foretime plenty of sage rulers and energetic
ministers, all benevolently inclined ? What had
come of it but this confusion ? Confucius (if Lao
Tzu ever heard of him) with his well-meaning and
tedious efforts at reform, might seem to crown a
line of futile endeavourers. Perhaps it was all a
mistake to try to control the people. Since coercion
brought evil, why not try the opposite method of
leaving men to the virtue of their inherent nature ?
After all, what did it matter ? Why not muse in
peace and quiet, contemplating this basic human
nature which was good ?

Lao Tzu is a puzzle. If one could be certain that
the *Tao-te-King* is his ! and if its translators only

---

[1] Notice those by Legge (*Sacred Books of the East*, Vol.
XXXIX), by de Harlez in *Annales de la Musée Guimet*, and by
Dr. Paul Carus (Open Court Pub. Co., Chicago, 1898).

agreed a little better ! We may be inclined to won-
der whether in the *Tao-te-King* the Chinese musing
spirit was not assisted by the spirit of the vine, a
very frequent aid to meditation in those old times.
These are queer sentences: "I alone appear listless
and still, as if my desires had not dawned; like an
infant which has not yet smiled; dejected, forlorn,
like one who has no home. I seem to be drifting
on the sea." This drifter knew at least to what
he would not tie himself, or direct his course by. It
should not be action, action taken with the purpose
of getting things, or impressing or compelling other
men. There had been too much of that! What
had the ruler's meddling ever brought but lawlessness ? And as for coercion, as for war — after an
army, briars and thorns spring up! Did some far
tradition come to Lao Tzu that the great sage-
rulers of the imagined past had done nothing, and
under them the people had thriven in blissful ignorance that there was a government ? As he tested
kindred thoughts in his own case, the principle of
inaction, with passivity, proved itself valid. He
found his kingdom within him: — without going
abroad, one understands; no need to look out of
the window to see the Tao of Heaven. "Let us
go," said someone, "and wander over the world."
"No," replied Lao Tzu, "the world is just as you see
it here."

Indeed, what is the use of learning many things ?

Better discard such knowledge and restless wisdom. It is the softest thing that overcomes the hardest. The advantage lies with inaction. Let one be as humble and non-assertive as water, always taking the lowest place.

A thoughtful man seeks to rest his temperamental convictions upon some absolute principle, at once sure and sufficing. Lao Tzu found such in an eternal unchanging root within the nature of man and behind the ways of Earth and Heaven. Thereupon all things became for him fundamentally the same, fundamentally one. Differences were but surface foolishness; complete inaction with respect to them approved itself as life's true rule. One can almost feel him groping after this changeless first beginning and eternal principle of all things, thus perhaps: "There was something undefined and complete, coming into existence before Heaven and Earth. How still it was and formless, standing alone, and undergoing no change, reaching everywhere and exhaustless. It may be regarded as the Mother of all things. I do not know its name, and I give it the designation of the Tao. . . . Man takes his law from the Earth; the Earth takes its law from Heaven; Heaven from the Tao. The law of the Tao is its being what it is." [1]

---

[1] *Tao-te-King*, 25. Is not this a far-off pre-natal echo of the One of Plotinus? The translator (Legge) felt doubtful of the last sentences.

Therein lay mystery, unapproachable, ineffable, not to be imparted. As the goodness of doing good is not the real good, so the Tao that can be attained, that can be trodden as the Path, is not the enduring and unchanging Tao. Evidently the name that can be named cannot be the name of the Enduring and Unchanging. This cannot be known and named so distinguishably: things distinguishable and namable are not the Tao.

Producing all things, the Tao strives not, clothing all as with a garment, yet not asserting itself as Lord; existing alike in the smallest and the greatest. Out of weakness, strength; thus it proceeds by contraries. Heaven and Earth, its grand embodiments, do not act from benevolence. They do not strive, yet always overcome; the meshes of Heaven's net are large, but let nothing escape. It lessens abundance, it supplements deficiency. Heaven shows no favour; it is always on the side of the good man.

Likewise the sage, says Lao Tzu, he who knows and holds the eternal Tao, will show no nepotism. The good he will meet with good, and what else has he within him with which to meet the bad? To embody and imitate the Tao was Lao Tzu's personal adjustment. As touching his effect on other men, Tao-like he would proceed by contraries, making no effort, renouncing sageness, discarding benevolence.

The Tao's way is plain — but the people love by-paths. The sage shall not even try to teach those in whom there may be no place for truth. He will do nothing, and the people will be transformed of themselves. All definitely directed effort departs from the purposeless indistinguishable effectiveness of Tao, and will result in the opposite of what is willed: out of law, lawlessness; out of the proprieties, disorder.

Not very clear and perhaps foolish, much of this *Tao-te-King!* Perhaps we have been barking up the wrong tree in following Lao Tzu, and the real game for us is Chuang Tzu after all — not Socrates but Plato. At all events, in Chuang Tzu, Chinese musing and indifference has metaphysical depth and wayward charm; he is not merely a puzzle, but a delight.

Artist as well as metaphysician, Chuang Tzu in his dialogues gives his arguments to various worthies, putting them even in the mouth of a somewhat apocryphal Confucius. In this he shares the faculty (one feels incompetent to proceed further with the comparison) of a Plato. One is embarrassed by his riches and his waywardness. He has also proved a hard nut to scholars,[1] and to the Chinese them-

[1] There are two English translations made with ripe knowledge; that of Legge in Vols. 39 and 40, *Sacred Books of the East*, and that of Herbert A. Giles (Quaritch, 1889). One who does not know Chinese may at least enjoy the delightful charm of the

selves, for whom he is more heretic than orthodox. He lived from the fourth into the third century before Christ, and a century or two later a Chinese historian compared his teachings to a flood which spreads at its own sweet will; consequently none could apply them to any definite use; they were too far-reaching. Long after, at the close of the Ming period, a Chinese commentator speaks appositely of his style: "The sudden statement and the sudden proof; the sudden illustration and the sudden reasoning; the decision, made to appear as no decision; the connexion, now represented as no connexion; the repetition, turning out to be no repetition : — these features come and go in the paragraphs like the clouds in the open firmament, changing every moment and delightful to behold. Some one describes it well: 'the guiding thread in the unspun floss; the snake sleeping in the grass.'" [1]

Chuang Tzu proceeds from Lao Tzu, or at all events represents a further stage in the progress of Chinese quietism and its justification. He stands upon the adjustment reached by his Master, but there he does not rest. The basis of this adjustment is the Tao. More clearly than his predecessor, Chuang Tzu

latter. It is the one from which I have taken my extracts, though with qualms over the differences between Prof. Giles and Dr. Legge.

[1] From Legge, *Sacred Books of the East*, Vol. 40, p. 275.

shows the Tao to be the transcendental root and core
of oneness beneath the apparent manifold of existence, and also the Norm of living for every creature.
With this conception of Tao as his basis, he shows
the relativity of qualities and the subjectivity of
concepts, also the folly of applying the measure of
one thing to the being or action of another. Proceeding further, he discloses the Identity of Contraries, and posits as a working principle the suppression of the silly phenomenal self with its passions
and desires, while he establishes the real eternal
Self as one with the Tao.[1] Thus Chuang Tzu's
adjustment, compared with Lao Tzu's, elaborates the
identification of Self with the Tao, and the identification of right living with the ways of the Tao's
aimless omnipotence.

These principles may be trite, their discussion
somewhat banal. But they came to Chuang Tzu
with the freshness of dawn, and made the matter
of delightful argument and the stimulus of dreams
dreamed with a purpose. Through this picturesque
argumentation let us track, if we can, his adjustment with life.

The monstrous Roc flying high above the earth
is as a mote in the sunbeam : after this and other
illustrations of the subjective relativity of times and
magnitudes, the argument turns to the identity of

[1] He reaches something like the conception of the Atman
Brahman in the Upanishads. Cf. post, Chapter III.

Subjective and Objective, the one emanating from the other; then to the blending of apparent contraries, which merge in an infinite One.

"Separation is the same as construction; construction is the same as destruction. Nothing is subject either to construction or to destruction, for these conditions are brought together into One. Only the truly intelligent understand this principle of the identity of all things. . . . But to wear out one's intellect in an obstinate adherence to the individuality of things, this is called *Three in the morning.*"

"What is *Three in the morning?*" exclaims someone.

"A keeper of monkeys," replies the speaker, "said with regard to their rations of chestnuts that each monkey was to have three in the morning and four at night. But at this the monkeys were very angry, so the keeper said they might have four in the morning and three at night; with which arrangement they were all well pleased. The actual number of the chestnuts remained the same, but there was an adaptation to the likes and dislikes of those concerned. Such is the principle of putting oneself into subjective relation with externals."

"There is nothing," continues the speaker after further interrogatories, "under the canopy of heaven greater than the tip of an autumn spikelet. A vast mountain is a small thing. Neither is there any age greater than that of a child cut off in infancy.

The universe and I came into being together; and I and everything therein are One."

At the end, the argument bathes in the mystery of life: "The revolutions of ten thousand years leave the Sage's Unity unscathed. . . . How do I know that love of life is not a delusion after all? How do I know but that he who dreads to die is not as a child who has lost the way and cannot find his home? . . . Some will even interpret the very dream they are dreaming; and only when they awake do they know it was a dream. By and by comes the Great Awakening, and then we find out that this life is really a great dream. Fools think they are awake now, and flatter themselves they know if they are really princes or peasants. Confucius and you are both dreams; and I who say you are dreams, — I am but a dream myself. . . . Once upon a time, I, Chuang Tzu, dreamt I was a butterfly, fluttering hither and thither. I was conscious only of following my fancies as a butterfly, and was unconscious of my individuality as a man. Suddenly I awaked, and there I lay, myself again. Now I do not know whether I was then a man dreaming I was a butterfly, or whether I am now a butterfly dreaming I am a man."

So much for relativity and the futility of apparent contraries, and so much for the mystery of it all. Chuang Tzu offers a different illustration of the folly of conventional human judgements in a chapter beginning thus: "It was the time of autumn floods. Every stream poured into the river which swelled in its turbid course. The banks receded so far from one another that it was impossible to tell a cow from a horse. Then the Spirit of the River laughed for joy that all the beauty of the earth was gathered to himself. Down with the stream he journeyed east, until he reached the ocean. There, looking eastwards and seeing no limit to its waves, his countenance changed. And as he gazed over the expanse, he sighed and said to the Spirit of the Ocean, 'A vulgar proverb says that he who has heard but part of the truth thinks no one equal to himself. And such a one am I. . . .'

"To which the Spirit of the Ocean replied, 'You cannot speak of ocean to a well-frog, the creature of a narrower sphere. You cannot speak of ice to a summer insect, the creature of a season. You cannot speak of Tao to a pedagogue; his scope is too restricted. But now that you have emerged from your narrow sphere and have seen the great ocean, I can speak to you of great principles.'" He then explains how vast the ocean is, and how trifling a thing it is in the Universe. But man, as compared with all creation, is as the tip of a hair upon a horse's skin.

"Very well," replied the Spirit of the River, "am I then to regard the universe as great and the tip of a hair as small?"

"Not at all," said the Spirit of the Ocean. "Dimensions are limitless; time is endless. Conditions are not invariable; terms are not final. Thus the wise man looks into space, and does not regard the small as too little, nor the great as too much; for he knows that there is no limit to dimension. He looks back into the past, and does not grieve over what is far off, nor rejoice over what is near, for he knows that time is without end. He investigates fulness and decay, and does not rejoice if he succeeds, nor lament if he fails; for he knows that conditions are not invariable. He who clearly apprehends the scheme of existence, does not rejoice over life, nor pine at death; for he knows that terms are not final."

The great man acts differently from others, but takes no credit, nor does he despise those who act otherwise. "Perfect virtue acquires nothing; the truly great man ignores self; this is the height of self-discipline. . . . From the point of view of Tao [the Spirit of the Ocean is speaking] there are no extremes of value or worthlessness. Men individually value themselves and hold others cheap. The world collectively withholds from the individual the right of appraising himself.

"If we say that a thing is great or small because it is relatively great or small, then there is nothing in all creation which is not great, nothing which is not small. . . . If we say that anything is good

D

or evil because it is either good or evil in our eyes, then there is nothing which is not good, nothing which is not evil. . . ."

"One might as well talk of the existence of heaven without that of earth, or of the negative principle without the positive. . . . Rulers have abdicated under different conditions, dynasties have been continued under different conditions. Those who did not hit off a favourable time and were in opposition to their age, they were called usurpers. Those who did hit off the right time and were in harmony with their age, they were called patriots. Fair and softly, my River Friend; what should you know of value and worthlessness, of great and small ?"

"In this case," replied the Spirit of the River, "what am I to do and what am I not to do ? How am I to arrange my declinings and receivings, my takings-hold and my lettings-go ?"

"From the point of view of Tao," said the Spirit of the Ocean, "value and worthlessness are like slopes and plains. . . . Tao is without beginning, without end. Other things are born and die. They are impermanent; and now for better, now for worse, they are ceaselessly changing form. Past years cannot be recalled; time cannot be arrested. The succession of states is endless; and every end is followed by a new beginning. Thus it may be said that man's duty to his neighbour is embodied in the eternal principles of the universe.

"The life of man passes by like a galloping horse, changing at every turn, at every hour. What should he do, other than let his decomposition go on?"

"If this is the case," retorted the Spirit of the River, "pray what is the value of Tao?"

"Those who understand Tao," answered the Spirit of the Ocean, "must necessarily apprehend the eternal principles above mentioned and be clear as to their application. Consequently, they do not suffer injury from without."

Much knowledge is a curse; one should know the inner principles. Chuang Tzu states his underlying doctrine thus: "At the beginning of the beginning, even Nothing did not exist. Then came the period of the Nameless. When One came into existence, there was One, but it was formless. When things got that by which they came into existence, it was called their virtue. That which was formless, but divided (*i.e.* allotted), though without interstice (unbroken in continuity) was called Destiny. Then came the movement which gave life, and things produced in accordance with the principles of life had what is called Form. When form encloses the spiritual part, each with its own characteristics, that is called its nature. By cultivating this nature, we are carried back to virtue; and if this is perfected, we become as all things were in the beginning. We become unconditioned, and the unconditioned is great."

Chuang Tzu, like Lao Tzu, represents the human need to grope for a foundation, upon which to stand with certainty of soul and freedom of action. When it is found, reliance upon one's principles is all that is needed, and acquiescence. Chuang Tzu sums up his own acquiescence (which was his adjustment to life) in a phrase several times repeated: "Tao gives me this form, this toil in manhood, this repose in old age, this rest in death. And surely that which is such a kind arbiter of my life is the best arbiter of my death."

Evidently one should immerse oneself in that essential virtue which lies far beneath the active manifestations of social relationships. This will be to keep oneself out of the web of conventional duties, free to muse and think and live within oneself and Tao. More fundamentally still it will consist in looking within for the real Tao-accordant Self, and in throwing off the passions and desires of the Self's surface entanglements. Such a life and such a Self will for the world express itself in categories of inaction.

This philosopher can put his principles picturesquely: When Chuang Tzu's wife died, a friend went to console, and found "the widower sitting on the ground, singing, with his legs spread out at a right angle, and beating time on a bowl." The

friend thinks self-restraint well enough, but this is
going too far.

"Not at all," replied Chuang Tzu; "when she
died, I could not help being affected by her death.
Soon, however, I remembered that she had already
existed in a previous state before birth, without
form or even substance; that while in that unconditioned condition, substance was added to spirit;
that this substance then assumed form; and that
the next stage was birth. And now by virtue of a
further change she is dead, passing from one phase
to another like the sequence of spring, summer,
autumn, and winter. And while she is thus lying
asleep in Eternity, for me to go about weeping and
wailing would be to proclaim myself ignorant of
these natural laws. Therefore I refrain."

Doubtless Chuang Tzu also had temperamental
preference for the principles which he held, — and
loved his freedom. He "was fishing in the Pu
when the prince of Chu sent two high officials to
ask him to take charge of the Chu State. Chuang
Tzu went on fishing, and without turning his head
said, 'I have heard that in Chu there is a sacred
tortoise which has been dead some three thousand
years, and that the prince keeps this tortoise care-
fully enclosed in a chest on the altar of his ancestral
temple. Now would this tortoise rather be dead
and have its remains venerated, or be alive and
wagging its tail in the mud ?'

"'It would rather be alive,' replied the two officials, 'and wagging its tail in the mud.'

"'Begone!' cried Chuang Tzu. 'I too will wag my tail in the mud.'"

Likewise Lao Tzu (in Chuang Tzu's book) shows explosively that virtue lies deeper than practice: "Confucius visited Lao Tzu, and spoke of charity and duty to one's neighbour. Lao Tzu said, 'The chaff from winnowing will blind a man's eyes so that he cannot tell the north from south. Mosquitoes will keep a man awake all night with their biting. And just in the same way this talk of charity and duty to one's neighbour drives me nearly crazy. Sir! I strive to keep the world to its own original simplicity. And as the wind bloweth where it listeth, so let Virtue establish itself. Wherefore such undue energy, as though searching for a fugitive with a big drum?'"

These philosophers not only believed, but reasoned in accordance with their principles, that "for the perfect man who is unavoidably summoned to power, there is naught like *Inaction*." This is how Chuang Tzu has Lao Tzu put it, when asked how men's hearts are to be kept in order without government: "Be careful," replied Lao Tzu, "not to interfere with the natural goodness of the heart of man. Man's heart may be forced down or stirred up. In each case the issue is fatal. By gentleness, the hardest heart may be softened. But try to cut and polish it, — 'twill glow like fire or freeze like ice. In the twinkling of an eye it will pass beyond the limits of the Four Seas. No bolt can bar, no bond can bind, — such is the human heart.

"Of old, the Yellow Emperor first caused charity and duty to one's neighbour to interfere with the natural goodness of the heart of man. In consequence of which, Yao and Shun wore the hair off their legs in endeavouring to feed their people. They disturbed their internal economy in order to find room for charity and duty to one's neighbour. They exhausted their energies in framing laws and statutes. Still they did not succeed." They endeavoured to coerce evil men, but the Empire continued in unrest. "By and by the Confucianists and the Mihists [another very moral sect] arose; and then came exultation, and anger of rivals, fraud between the simple and the cunning, recrimination between the virtuous and the evil, slander between the honest and the dishonest, until decadence set in, men fell away from their original virtue, their natures became corrupt, and there was a general rush for knowledge.

"The next thing was to coerce by all kinds of physical torture, thus bringing utter confusion into the Empire, the blame for which rests upon those who would interfere with the natural goodness of the heart of man. In consequence, virtuous men sought refuge in mountain caves, while rulers of

States sat trembling in their ancestral halls. Then when dead men lay about pillowed on each other's corpses, when cangued prisoners and condemned criminals jostled each other in crowds, then the Confucianists and the Mihists, in the midst of gyves and fetters, stood forth to preach! . . . Therefore I said, abandon wisdom and discard knowledge, and the Empire will be at peace."

Our old friend Lao Tzu had a fit disciple, who "alone had attained to the Tao of his master. He lived up north on the Wei-lei Mountains. Of his attendants he dismissed those who were systematically clever or conventionally charitable. The useless remained with him; the incompetent served him. And in three years the district of Wei-lei was greatly benefited."

A final statement of the matter perhaps is touched with a slight sneer: "The difficulty of governing lies in the inability to practise self-effacement."

Likewise for the individual; let him too practise self-effacement, effacement, that is to say, of particular desires, passions, anxieties, and efforts. Chuang Tzu illuminates this with one of his best narrative-disquisitions: A wise man with an un-rememberable name "paid a visit to the prince of Lu. The latter wore a melancholy look; whereupon the philosopher inquired what was the cause.

"'I study the doctrines of the ancient Sages,' replied the prince, 'I carry on the work of my predecessors. I respect religion. I honour the good. Never for a moment do I relax in these points; yet I cannot avoid misfortune, and consequently I am sad.'

"'Your Highness' method of avoiding misfortune,' said the philosopher, 'is but a shallow one. A handsome fox or a striped leopard will live in a mountain forest, hiding beneath some cliff. This is their repose. They come out by night and keep in by day. This is their caution. Though under the stress of hunger and thirst, they lie hidden, hardly venturing to slink to the river bank in search of food. This is their resoluteness. Nevertheless, they do not escape the misfortune of the net and the trap. But what crime have they committed? 'Tis their skin which is the cause of their trouble; and is not the State of Lu your Highness' skin? I would have your Highness put away body and skin alike, and cleansing your heart and purging it of passion, betake yourself to the land where mortality is not (*i.e.* Tao). . . . Thither would I have your Highness proceed, power discarded, and the world left behind, only putting trust in Tao.'

"'The road is long and dangerous,' said the prince. 'Rivers and hills to be crossed, and I without boat or chariot;—what then?'

"'Unhindered by body and unfettered in mind, your Highness will be a chariot to yourself.'

"'But the road is long and dreary, and unin-

habited. I shall have no one to turn to for help;
and how, without food, shall I ever be able to get
there ?'"

"'Decrease expenditure (of energy) and lessen
desires,' answered the philosopher, 'and even though
without provisions, there will be enough. And
then through river and over sea your Highness will
travel into shoreless illimitable space. From the
borderland, those who act as escort will return;
but thence onwards your Highness will travel far.
It is the human in ourselves which is our hindrance;
and the human in others which causes sorrow.
And I would have your Highness put off this hindrance and rid yourself of this sorrow, and roam
with Tao alone through the realms of Infinite
Nought.'"

It is also taught consistently in Chuang Tzu's
book that neither man's life nor his individuality
is his own, being in either case the delegated harmony and adaptability of the spiritual powers constituting it.

"Man passes through this sublunary life as a
white horse passes a crack. Here one moment,
gone the next. One modification brings life; then
another, and it is death. Living creatures cry out;
human beings sorrow. The bow-sheath is slipped
off; the clothes-bag is dropped; and in the confusion the soul wings its flight, and the body follows, on the great journey home!

"The reality of the formless, the unreality of that which has form, — this is known to all. Those who are on the road to attainment care not for these things, but the people at large discuss them. Attainment implies non-discussion! Manifested, Tao has no objective value; hence silence is better than argument. It cannot be translated into speech; better, then, say nothing at all. This is called the great attainment."

Much of this argumentation, if such it be, or personal adjustment, has meaning and appeal, or has it not, according as one may take it, or perhaps, according as one is constituted. Thus it may be either appealing or foolish. The way lies near to an exposition of the real Self which might seem to have come out of the Indian Upanishads: "That Self is eternal; yet all men think it mortal; That Self is infinite; yet all men think it finite. Those who possess Tao are princes in this life and rulers in the hereafter. Those who do not possess Tao behold the light of day in this life, and become clods of earth in the hereafter."

One sees that Chuang Tzu's philosophy is held within his adjustment with life. The philosopher himself is still human, can recognize half humorously his own imbecility and occasional falling away from his principles, as in this story: Wandering in a park, he saw a strange bird with great wings, which flew close past his head to alight in a chestnut grove.

"What manner of bird is this?" cried Chuang Tzu. "With strong wings it does not fly away; with large eyes it does not see."

So he picked up his skirts and strode towards it with his cross-bow, anxious to get a shot. Just then he saw a cicada enjoying itself in the shade, forgetful of all else. And he saw a mantis spring and seize it, forgetting in its act its own body, which the strange bird immediately pounced upon and made its prey. And this it was which had caused the bird to forget its own nature.

"Alas!" cried Chuang Tzu with a sigh, "how creatures injure one another. Loss follows the pursuit of gain." So he laid aside his bow and went home, driven away by the parkkeeper, who wanted to know what business he had there.

After this he did not quit his house for three months, till a disciple, wondering, asked why. "While keeping my physical frame," replied Chuang Tzu, "I lost sight of my real self. Gazing at muddy water, I lost sight of the clear abyss. Now when I strolled into the park, I forgot my real self. That strange bird which flew close past me to the chestnut grove, forgot its nature. The keeper of the chestnut grove took me for a thief. Consequently I have not been out."

No, he had rather dwell within his house, within himself. How clearly he could lay aside non-essentials and cast himself upon the elements of his being, is shown in the final scene: "When Chuang Tzu was about to die, his disciples expressed a wish to give him a splendid funeral. But Chuang Tzu said, 'With Heaven and Earth for my coffin and shell, with the sun, moon and stars as my burial regalia; and with all creation to escort me to the grave, — are not my funeral paraphernalia ready to hand?'

"'We fear,' argued the disciples, 'lest the carrion kite should eat the body of our master'; to which, Chuang Tzu replied, 'Above ground, I shall be food for kites; below, I shall be food for mole-crickets and ants. Why rob one to feed the other?'"

Thus it was for this man who knew: "Birth is not a beginning; death is not an end. There is existence without limitation; there is continuity without a starting point. Existence without limitation is Space. Continuity without a starting point is Time. There is birth, there is death, there is issuing forth, there is entering in. That through which one passes in and out without seeing its form, that is the Portal of God — which is non-existence, from which all things spring."

As certain also of your own poets have said:

"Our birth is but a sleep and a forgetting."

CHAPTER III

THE INDIAN ANNIHILATION OF INDIVIDUALITY

INDIAN thinking is driven by a temperamental need of adjustment with the Infinite, and by a temperamental aversion for the incessant round of life and death. The adjustments attained were shaped through a tenacious dialectic; yet they were impelled by the Indian yearning for emancipation from impermanence and recurrent death. By the close of the fifth century before Christ, cognate and complementary solutions had been reached, which were religious and also metaphysical. These solutions affected the spiritual destinies of Asia. They were, moreover, in their intellectual bearings representative of the opposite positions regarding men and things in which philosophers in various lands have always tended to range themselves. The Brahman-Atman doctrines of the Upanishads and the teachings of Buddhism which seemingly rose out of them, by the way of dissent if not of revolution, present opposite poles of thought. The Brahman pole points to an Absolute All-One, empirically unknowable, but felt religiously, and demonstrated as metaphysical verity. Vaguely it was to be lived unto as a religious goal, and patterned upon as a norm of conduct. The Buddhist solution refused assent to any Absolute, which of a certainty could not be found in the changing world and the passing experience of man.

Yet transience and change were as intolerable to one Indian phase of thought as to the other; and the Buddha preaches emancipation from phenomenal life as earnestly as if behind there lay an Absolute instead of Nought. But these opposite poles in India are not in all respects distinguishable. The Absolute of the Upanishads does not differ practically from Nought, but only metaphysically. In other systems, however, away from India, Being or the Supreme Being is the antithesis of Nought in many further modes, and one may fruitfully reflect upon the different motives, the different processes, and the different goals of supreme desire, or its seeming renunciation, which have drawn men to one conclusion or the other in company, shall we say, with Yajnavalkya or Gotama, with Plato or Heracleitus, with Christ or with Apollyon.

There have always been men to despise or condemn the lures of life, although their condemnation has proceeded along different lines of misprisal. Some have been moved by fear of sin, some by the sorrow of impermanence, and some by contempt for whatever does not share in the steadfastness of

the conceptions of the mind. The Indian misprisal united the last two reasons, and was a thing
of mood as well as thought. Conversely, the higher
Indian modes of spiritual freedom were harmonies
of mood and argument.

After what one is prone to call the Vedic age of
probable Aryan advance and conquest in India,
the thoughtful men of the succeeding generations
gave themselves over to profound, if not the happiest,
meditation. The remark of the Greek observer
Megasthenes, who visited India in the train of
Alexander, that the Indian sages, — forest dwellers
he calls them — think much on death, would have
applied centuries before his time. Many of those
temperamentally motived philosophic treatises which
are called Upanishads and are attached as appen-
dices and reconsiderations to the Vedic literature,
are earlier than the fifth century before Christ,
presumably and probably, for dates are never certain in India. They consider death inordinately (as
we might say, if we chose to forget our own monkish
literature), and present the ancient Brahmanical
adjustment of the human spirit — with life and
the universe ? yes, perhaps; but it were more to
the point to speak of this adjustment as an emancipation of the soul from death, and constantly recurring death.

To anyone who would extract a system from
them, these Upanishads will prove tangled paths.

Yet the topics of discussion throughout are much the same, and the general tenor of the solutions. There is frequent dialogue, question and answer, with youths and kings and Brahmans for speakers. It would be interesting, were it justifiable, to attach the argumentation to the name of some ancient and dramatic Brahman, like Yajnavalkya. And perhaps it may be well to follow closely some instance of his dramatic arguments, if only to illustrate vividly the point that the Upanishads form a huge attempt, or series of attempts, to bring peace and freedom to the anxious human spirit, emancipate the soul from death, and possibly win for it eternal felicity.

Belief in the transmigration of souls is either inculcated or assumed. Therefore the soul has to be freed from its torment of rebirth and redeath. This goal is reached through mazes of symbolism and metaphysics intended to establish the Absolute All-One, and identify the Soul, the Self, with It, — the Atman with Brahman. For the Atman is this Absolute Self within each one of us, if we will but know it; and Brahmă, a word which in the Vedas had meant prayer, has at length through turns of monstrous symbolism and subjectivity, been transformed to that prayer which has worked its own fulfilment, which has not merely reached but has *become* its own uttermost desire, the unchanging and imperishable Absolute. The Self is That;

E

That is the Self; and beyond it there is Nought; only *Maya*, the delusion of Name and Form.

This Absolute is to be attained through enlightenment; by knowing it and desiring nothing else. But can it be known? Yes and no. It cannot be known by observation, perhaps not in consciousness in any way. Will the path of cumulative predication lead to It?—It is this, and that and everything, the One within the Many: and this, and that, and everything art Thou. Negation may prove the surer way; for neither that, nor this nor anything is It. It cannot be known through restless tossings, but only dreamlessly. Where then is consciousness? Has that too vanished in this dreamless knowledge? He who has realized Brahman, and that the Self is It, for him there will be no desire in this life, and no rebirth unto redeath; for him it will be true, as Yajnavalkya declares: "There is no consciousness after death."

Listen to Yajnavalkya speaking with his wife Maitreyi, as he is about to enter the final seclusion of the forest; he will divide his goods between her and another wife. Maitreyi stops him: "If the wealth of the whole earth belonged to me, would it make me immortal?"

"No," replied Yajnavalkya, "like the life of rich people will be thy life; there is no hope of immortality by wealth."

"What should I do with that by which I do not

become immortal? That which my Lord knoweth, tell to me."

Yajnavalkya replied: "Come, thou that art truly dear to me, sit down and I will explain it to thee. Verily a husband is dear not for the husband's sake, but for the Self's sake: likewise wife, sons, kingdoms, the world and all the gods, these are dear, not for their own, but for the Self's sake; in order that thou mayest love the Self alone. We should meditate upon the Self. He who has seen, heard and known the Self, knows the Universe. He who looks for anything save in the Self will be deluded, — as if he should seek for the notes of lute or drum beyond the instrument producing them! And as when a fire is laid with damp wood, clouds of smoke are spread around, so from this great Being has all knowledge and doctrine been breathed forth. It is the meeting-place of all forms, as waters meet in the ocean, sounds in the ear, colours in the eye, and perceptions in the mind. And as a lump of salt, dissolved in water, cannot be taken out, and the water will always taste salt, so this great Being which is all knowledge, vanishes in the elements from which it rises. There is no consciousness after death."

"Now thou hast bewildered me," said Maitreyi.

"O Maitreyi, I say nothing that is bewildering. For when there is *as it were* duality, then one sees the other, one smells the other, one hears the other, one salutes the other, one perceives and knows the other. But when the Self is all this, how should He see another, hear another, salute another, or perceive and know another? How should He know Him by whom He knows all this? That Self is to be described by No, No! He is incomprehensible, for he cannot be comprehended; he cannot perish; he does not attach himself; unfettered, he does not suffer. How, O beloved, should he know the knower? Thus, O Maitreyi, thou hast been instructed." When he had thus spoken, Yajnavalkya went away into the forest.[1]

Note the "as it were" of this last passage — duality, manifoldness, only *as it were*, not really. The Atman-Brahman is the sole reality; it is the All; it is free from desire, it is also essentially unknowable, for it is You. Knowledge of this is in itself emancipation, and looses the soul from the delusions of rebirth. "He who is without desire, desire having been laid to rest, is himself his own desire — he is Brahman." So spake Yajnavalkya.

The Upanishads throughout their repetitious involutions do not flinch from the principle of emancipation through non-desire. Yet they seem to flicker down from these pale heights of Yajnavalkya; and through concessions to the insistent calls of

[1] Condensed from *Brihadaranyaka-Upanishad*, II, 4 and IV, 5, mainly as rendered by Max Müller, *Sacred Books of the East*, Vol. XV, with emendations from Deussen.

empirical knowledge, the Atman-Brahman becomes more active, more cosmogonic if one will, and more knowable. It fills the rôles of Creator, Preserver, and Destroyer — "the womb of nature and perhaps her grave." "At the bidding of this imperishable one, O Gargi (again speaks Yajnavalkya) sun and moon are kept asunder, heaven and earth are kept asunder; the minutes and the hours are kept asunder, the days and nights, the months and seasons and the years. At the bidding of this imperishable one, O Gargi, the streams run from the snow mountains, some to the east and some to the west, whithersoever each goes. At the bidding of this imperishable one, men praise the bountiful givers, the gods desire the sacrificer, the fathers the offerings to the dead." [1]

It is thus that to the high strain of that adjustment which lies in the dreamless Unity of the Absolute, the Upanishads add props and comfortings, sops to the insistent barkings of man's actual environment. Yet they still teach unwaveringly the emancipation lying in detachment and freedom from desire.

Religion attaches itself by the ways of hope and aspiration to aims and objects which may or may not prove clear and consistent when critically analysed. Logic and metaphysics, issuing from

[1] *Brih.-Up.* III, 8, 9 (Deussen).

other phases of human faculty, are likely to devi-
talise the objects of religious yearning. In ratioci-
nation the religious impulse is checked, its emotion
distracted, while the seamy sides of the method
and Object of Religion are disclosed. Other
emotions, arising in the progress of debate, may
confirm the combatants' positions; but they are
the emotions of conflict. The creators of religions
are those who have voiced anew men's yearnings
and given new life to their hopes, and with such
sufficiency of definiteness that others could take up
the impulse and echo its expression, — an expression, an actualisation, mark you, of their own poten-
tialities of aspiration.

The most ancient Buddhist writings are in Pali,
a language current in parts of northern India about
the time when Gotama lived, in the fifth or sixth
century before Christ. If they are tediously
dialectical, they still deprecate the discussion of
whatever goes beyond salvation's needs; and though
the argumentative form seems to point backward
to the actual methods of Gotama, one may be sure
that he brought again to true expression those Indian aspirations and those notes of Indian sorrow
which had been over dialecticised in the Upanishads. A comfort deeper than argument drew men
to the Buddha, and evoked their cry: "I take refuge
in the Buddha, in his Teaching, and in the Brotherhood." There is in fact no ground for questioning

what is vouched for by the concurrence of all the early records : that as the adjustment which Gotama reached was reached through meditation, so he set it forth in the form of reasoned statements which made their own transforming and vitalising use of the Brahmanical argumentation of his time.

Gotama's attainment and the whole content of the Buddha's system, which from pity he imparted to those who were fit for wisdom, may, from our point of view, be bounded within the conception of the individual's adjustment with life. The circumstances of the attainment of this noble Sakya youth to Buddhahood have been told, usually with an accumulation of myth, millions of times. Shall we say, the tale is the more impressive the more nakedly it is presented in the closest approximation to the probable facts ? There is profound absurdity in this idea : the probable facts ! they were of the spirit in its crisis and in its preparation too. With scarcely less foolishness might one seek for the "probable facts" of the Forty Days in the wilderness or the night upon Gethsemane ! Possibly the myth-making instinct of the Buddha's followers has wisely adorned the tale, in order that it might symbolise the ineffable value of this achievement for mankind. Alack ! this reverent mythopoesy is only too apt to be fond and foolish : in India it has done as foolishly in Birthstories of the Buddha's countless previous lives, as

it was to do in our apocryphal Gospels, filling out
the child-life of Jesus to accord with the imperative
silliness of the human mind. Only let us be also
sure that any attempt to discover the truth of
such experiences, through critical weighings of the
sources, is a process likely to fool the wise more
dangerously than legends fool the babes.

Gotama was born and lived in northeastern India.
His temper was impregnated with the moods, and
his mind was filled with the thoughts, which are
expressed in the Upanishads. He was a child of
the Indian discussion of the Absolute and Unabso-
lute, and the Indian aversion to the phenomena of
life. His system drew its manner, its setting, most
of the substance of its argument, — or by repulsion
its denials — from the spiritual environment of its
founder. Its point of view, its temper, its purpose
are practically those of Brahmanism. Said the
young Brahman to Death : "Keep thou thy horses,
keep dance and song for thyself. Shall we be happy
with these things, seeing thee ?" [1] "How is there
laughter," says the Buddhist, "how is there joy, as
the world is always burning ? Why do ye not seek
a light, ye who are surrounded by darkness ? This
body is wasted, full of sickness and frail; this heap
of corruption breaks to pieces, life indeed ends in
death." "Let no man love anything; loss of the

[1] *Katha-Up.* i, I, 26.

beloved is evil. Those who love nothing and hate nothing have no fetters. From love comes grief, from love comes fear; he who is free from love knows neither grief nor fear." [1] Buddhism, finally, is at one with Brahman doctrine, in teaching that ignorance is the ground of human misery, while in knowledge lies salvation.

But in its metaphysics and psychology, Buddhism was revolutionary, denying the Absolute Brahman and the Absolute Self in man. It was also revolutionary in abjuring caste and abandoning sacrifices along with asceticism.

Who does not know the outline of external circumstance, fairly historical, enveloping Gotama's attainment to the Buddhahood ? This highborn youth of the Sakya people marries, begets a son, and as the years leave him the graver for their passage, he abandons his home and becomes an ascetic "in the forest." It was not unusual for a man thus to seek detachment and salvation; and Gotama came in search of this adjustment.

He practised asceticism, it is said, for seven years. Apparently gaining no help from his austerities, he stopped them. At this evident relapse, five ascetics who had been his followers left him — alone. One night he perceived, we are told, the universal principle of the causation and dependency

---

[1] *Dhammapada*, 146, 148, 211, 215.

of all phenomena relating to man, or constituting states of human consciousness; thereupon realising the pain of everything pertaining to individual life, he was loosed from the craving which is sorrow, and entails rebirth. This was his adjustment. Having attained the peace of complete enlightenment, he became the Buddha, or as he later called himself, the Tathāgata — the perfected one.

Gotama's adjustment with life, the enlightenment through which he became the Buddha, consisted of this principle of dependency and causation, and of the contents of the more practical working formulæ of the Eightfold Path and the Four Noble Truths. The Eightfold Path and the Four Truths, according to the concurrent testimony of the early records, made the kernel of his teaching when addressing those whose minds were open. When they had received this instruction, he would impart more fundamentally the difficult principle of causation and dependency. To the intellectual mood of which Buddha was the exponent, everything embraced within the cravings of individuality, in fact all states of human consciousness, were painful; blessedness lay in release: that was Salvation. It was this path of happy release which he set forth to his disciples, and upon which he himself had entered by the way of the principle of causation and dependency. This expressed his understanding of life's painful round — the giro of consciousness — and the manner of release. Let us therefore consider it, before referring to the embodiment of the teacher's doctrine in his current preaching.

Buddha did not state his principle of causation in the categories of western thinking, nor did he ever expound it in a way that we can deem satisfactory. Attempts to present it to our minds seem to become more futile as they become more analytic and explicit. One may as well admit that it cannot be made quite clear, nor accommodated to our ways of thinking, without introducing much that the Buddha did not intend. But at all events the scheme is striking, and impresses where it may not convince or satisfy.

Gotama did not learn of pain in the forest, for the realisation of it had driven him from his home. In the forest, he gained insight into the way of its origin and cessation. But since all life was filled with pain, insight into its origin and cessation involved enlightenment as to the origin and cessation of all experience entering human consciousness. So questions of origination, coming to pass, becoming, of passing away, cessation, and release, pressed on his mind; the solution raised Gotama to Buddhahood. Here it is — in its Englished inexpressibility.

"In dependence upon ignorance arise the Sankhārā (conformations, Gestaltungen, a term which will fit itself into no single European word — or many European words); in dependence upon them

arises consciousness; in dependence upon consciousness arise name and corporeal form (or mind
and body); from name and form spring the six
fields (*i.e.* the senses, which include *thought* as a
sixth); from them comes contact (between the
senses and their objects); from contact springs sensation (or feeling); from sensation springs thirst
(or desire); from thirst springs grasping or clinging
(to individual existence); from grasping springs
becoming (or possibly the predisposition to becoming); from that comes birth (perhaps rather rebirth); and in dependence upon birth follow old
age and death, grief, lamentation, suffering, dejec-
tion and despair. Such is the origin of the whole
realm of pain."

This being the origin of pain, release lay in the
counter truth; and thus the Buddha supplemented
his principle of dependent origination by that of
cessation on the removal of the cause: "But, if
ignorance be removed through the complete destruction of desire, this effects a removal of the
Sankhārā; through their removal, consciousness
ceases; by the cessation of consciousness, name and
form will cease; thereupon the fields of sense fall
away; then there is no contact, sensation ceases,
thirst is destroyed and with it falls the grasping
after existence; thereupon becoming ceases and
birth (or rebirth); and old age and death and the
whole realm of sorrow are destroyed."

Again be it said, it is futile to discuss the incidents of this scheme of causal or conditioned *taking place;* there is, as will be seen, no *being* in it.   But we may realise that Gotama, affected by current doctrines of transmigration, did not think of any life as beginning at birth and ending at death; and we shall fail to understand this causal scheme unless we feel it lapping over from one living to the next. In Brahmanism that which passes over is the soul held in the destiny of its desires and deeds.   In Buddhism this entity of soul is dissipated, and it is the power of the act (Karma) which carries over, and somehow impregnates a new consciousness and imposes itself upon name and form anew.   The "ignorance" appearing as the first in the chain of evil, means ignorance of the Buddha's teachings, especially as set forth in the Eightfold Path and the Four Noble Truths.

The early stories tell of the Buddha's hesitancy to impart to purblind men the adjustment which had brought him peace at last, after such years of meditation.   At last from goodness, from pity, or from a complexity of benignant or functional motives escaping our analysis, and difficult for us to reconcile with Buddha's doctrine, he decides to preach.   So he sets out to instruct those five ascetics who had been his followers until repelled by his abandonment of asceticism.   Perhaps in view of their cavillings, this famous sermon of the eight-

fold path and four truths, first spoken as men say
in the deer-park Isapatana at Benares, is, in some
versions, made to open thus:

"There are two extremes which he who has
given up the world ought to avoid: a life given to
pleasures and lusts, which is degrading, sensual,
vulgar and profitless; and a life given to mortifica-
tions, which is painful, ignoble and profitless. By
avoiding these two extremes the Tathāgata has
gained knowledge of the Middle Path, which leads
to insight and wisdom, to peace and to Nirvana.
It is the way to the abatement of suffering, the Holy
Eightfold Path of Right Belief, Right Decision,
Right Speech, Right Act, Right Life, Right Endeavour, Right Thought, and Right Meditation.

"This, ye Monks, is the noble truth of suffering:
Birth is suffering, age is suffering, sickness is suffering, death is suffering, the presence of the unloved,
the absence of the loved, is suffering, not to obtain
our desire is suffering; in fine, the fivefold clinging
to existence is suffering.

"This, ye monks, is the noble truth of the Origin
of Suffering: it is the thirst that leads from rebirth
to rebirth, with pleasure and lust finding its delight
here and there: thirst for pleasure, for becoming,
for the transitory.

"This, ye monks, is the holy truth of the Cessation of Suffering: the cessation of thirst through
the complete destruction of desire, letting it go,

abjuring it, freeing oneself from it, giving it no place.

"This, ye monks, is the holy truth of the Way of the Cessation of Suffering: it is the Holy Eight-fold Path of right faith, right resolve, right speech, right act, right life, right effort, right thought, right meditation."

One has here the outline of the Buddha's adjustment and calming of the spirit, into reconciliation, into peace made perfect — into blessedness. One notices, moreover, that his entire doctrine, what he attained for himself, and what he preached to others, is essentially adjustment, religion one may call it. Gotama certainly had a mind of power. Prodigious mental effort was involved in carrying through such an analysis of the origination, dependence and extinction of the chain of individual consciousness, the virtual sum total of what we know and feel, what we conceivably have been and are becoming. The result, partly derived, partly original, and, as a whole, constructive, was a law universal and not to be escaped from, the law of the effect or power of the Act, whether mental or realised in deeds. This reaches through all conscious or sentient living, from the insect to the perfected disciple about to attain Nirvana. It was a wonderful explanatory scheme of the origin and course of individuality, with its cravings to realise itself on and on; a scheme forming the dialectic basis of the religion or doctrine of the way to blessed release from the successive stages of an existence made up of suffering.

Suffering — that is the question. How does one think and feel about life as he has experienced it ? Does one like or dislike it on the whole, feel it to be desirable or intolerable ? Before Gotama's birth the meditative temper of India had pronounced against life's transient round, and had cast itself upon the endeavour to construct a refuge, a state, a being, freed from conditions of origination and cessation, set beyond change and suffering, and winnowed from all elements of *becoming*. The result had been the superconscious Brahman-Atman, the absolute being, and the corresponding announcement of Yajnavalkya, there is no consciousness after death for the completed and desireless sage.

Gotama likewise sought, and as the Buddha attained, release from that chain of individuality and craving which was suffering, and which was also a ceaseless becoming; but he perceived no Absolute in which to share, nor any sure unalterable Self. Consequently when the suffering, when the becoming, is stopped, is there anything beyond the blessedness of release ?

If the Buddha's life-adjustment included the answer to this query, we do not know it, — he did not impart it to his disciples. He had reached the way of release from suffering, a path of peace, which may be entered on even before death. He refused to say whether the Tathāgata and other perfected ones would or would not exist thereafter. Nor would he solve the question of an ego or no-ego, whether there was any being within the universal process of becoming. Far less would he enter on a discussion as to whether the world was finite or infinite, eternal or perishable. Such discussions were as if a man, shot with a poisoned arrow, should delay its removal till he had learned the name and city of him who had drawn the bow, or whether the arrow was feathered from the wings of a hawk or a vulture. The religious life, leading to the blessed release, did not depend on answering such questions. Sufficeth to know how bodily form arises and perishes, how sensation, perception, predispositions, and consciousness arise, and how they perish. This is the knowledge which brings deliverance.[1] The Buddha is many times reported to have said, "As the great ocean has but one taste, the taste of salt, so my doctrine has but one flavour, the flavour of emancipation."

So he stopped with the great adjustment; and with teaching a way of life and accordant precepts for conduct enabling men to attain it. He evinces no detached and disinterested pursuit of knowledge:

[1] Cf. H. C. Warren, *Buddhism in Translations*, §13, pp. 117–127. (Harvard Oriental Series, Fifth Issue, 1909.)

F

his adjustment had involved enough of wrestling with life's data; to have gone further would have extended needlessly the sorrow-filled states of human consciousness. We may say that a pursuit of knowledge here and there would have countered the very principles of his adjustment; but then likely we shall be talking in terms of our own, and not in his. Doubtless Buddha never put the matter in this way; and how, if in any way, he put it, we do not know.

It was enough. He had won peace; and having won it, he lived on and taught it to the brotherhood, putting it probably to the more enlightened in those same self-reliant reasonings in which he had won it for himself. To attain to this emancipating knowledge, and conform one's thought and conduct to its principles, was sufficient *disciplina* to fill the most strenuous life. The path to be trodden by the disciples of the Buddha was not less arduous than the path to be trodden by the disciples of the Christ. And when the Tathāgata had passed away, no aid, beyond the inspiration of his example, remained for those Buddhist monks who would attain the blessedness of peace. They were cast upon their own endeavours. So he had adjured them, "Be ye lamps unto yourselves. Be ye a refuge unto yourselves. Betake yourselves to no external refuge. Hold fast to the truth as a lamp. Look not for a refuge to anyone beside yourselves. Let a monk as he dwells in the body so regard the body that he being strenuous, thoughtful and mindful, may whilst in the world overcome the grief which arises from the bodily craving; so also, as he thinks, or reasons, or feels, let him overcome the grief which arises from the craving due to ideas, or to reasoning, or to feeling. . . . Behold now, I exhort you, saying, Decay is inherent in all things. Work out your own salvation with diligence. These were the last words of the Perfected One." [1]

[1] Book of the Great Decease, *Sacred Books of the East*, Vol. XI.

CHAPTER IV

ZARATHUSHTRA

A STRIKINGLY non-Indian and militant adjustment was achieved by a man of kindred race, Zarathushtra, the prophet of Iran.[1] He won his spiritual freedom through creating a new faith and consecrating himself to a chosen cause, the faith and cause of Mazda. He had found no peace in the worship of his people's gods. Apparently they had become to him abominations. His peace required a god who could satisfy his intellect and moral consciousness; and his nature cried for a mighty righteous One to whom his heart might turn and whom his strength might serve; who in return would bring efficient aid and the victory that was alike his and his servant's.

Zarathushtra would have found no rest in the nature-gods and wavering symbolism of the Indian pantheon, nor in an unresponsive Absolute, nor in such a godless gospel of relief from sorrow as the

[1] Cf. A. V. W. Jackson, "Zoroaster the Prophet of Ancient Iran" (1899), also, James Hope Moulton, "Early Zoroastrianism," Hibbert Lectures for 1912. The date and birthplace of Zarathushtra are not known. He may have lived as late as the sixth century before Christ, or as early as the tenth. And where in Persia or Media (Atropatene ?) he was born is also unknown.

Buddha preached.   There is utter disparity between Indian convictions and the Zarathushtrian temper. Is it that travelling north and westward, crossing the Hindukush, we have come to a new spiritual atmosphere ?   We have certainly left the region of Taoism's anæmic inaction and the heaven-approved ethics of Confucius.   Nor do we find conceptions of a still and fathomless relationship with the divine, as of Atman and Brahman, nor any self-reliant, godless, scheme of quenching the thirst, the suffering, and the consciousness of man.

One feels the futility of placing Confucianism, Brahmanism, Buddhism, along with the fighting faiths of Zarathushtra and the Hebrew prophets, under the same general concept of religion; likewise the futility of separating the intellectual from the practical driving elements within these systems; and finally the dangers besetting the attempt to draw broad lines between them and the inquiring intellectualism of Greek philosophy.   Beneath all systems lies the universal need of human nature to function according to its faculties, while the differences inhering in those faculties and arising through their exercise involve the whole human complex, and will not lie snug on separate shelves of ethics, religion, philosophy.

How the motives vary with the tempers of the men ! All great exponents of the human need of adjustment, masters likewise of the rational and emotional faculties through which that need is satisfied, seek to learn and know; but with such different inspiration and in such different fields. Perhaps those who are entitled to the name of philosopher would learn for knowledge's sake; but with equal ardour the founders of ethical or religious systems have sought in knowledge a rational basis for their working principles and a justification for their ideals, — only with what a tumult of diversity they move! These great ones, moreover, approve or inculcate like ways of conduct — benevolence, truth, respect for others' rights, the virtues on which society everywhere must stand. Yet how the sanction or reason for the practice of these virtues varies! Indeed, so great is the diversity both of motive and intellectual energy that one is equally impressed by the sameness of the under-lying need to function and the heterogeneous modes, the temperamental diversity, of its manifestation.

Zarathushtra was a man hard-pressed between the resistance of opponents and his own impulse to fight and make others fight for the faith which moved him. He comes close to the Hebrew prophets in the temper of his life-adjustment. This begins in reflection and prayer, rises to a sense of divine call, and completes itself in consecration of his energies to the cause of Mazda. The fiery lines of thought along which Zarathushtra may be deemed to have broken from the beliefs about him and to have set

as his star the mental vision of Ahura Mazda, are
suggested in the *Gathas:* [1]

"With outspread hands I will pray, O Mazda,
to fulfil all the works of the good spirit, that I may
please Good Thought. . . . I who would serve
thee, O Mazda, — grant me the blessings of the two
worlds, that of the body and that of the spirit, by
which Ahura places in happiness them that delight
him; I who give myself to thee, O Righteousness,
and to Good Thought, and to Ahura Mazda, to
whom belong imperishable dominion . . . come at
my call to my help. I who through Good Thought,
and knowing the rewards of Mazda, will while I
have strength teach men to seek the good. . . .
Come with Good Thought and Righteousness, O
Mazda by thy sure words give mighty and enduring
help to Zarathushtra."

Hard upon such thought of Ahura and the
thinker's ardour to bring to pass Good Thought and
the divine Righteousness, comes the call. It is as
when Isaiah beheld Yahweh high and lifted up,
heard the "Holy, Holy, Holy!" and the words,
"Whom shall I send?" to which not alone his lips
but his life answered, "Send me!" So the life of
Zarathushtra responded to the nature and com-

---

[1] The portions of the Zend-Avesta known as the *Gathas*
(*Yasna*, 28–34, 43–51, 53) are the most direct evidence we have
of Zarathushtra's thought. But the translations are still difficult,
if not uncertain.

mands of Ahura Mazda. He is speaking as from a later period in his life:

"And I knew thee as an holy one, Ahura Mazda, when Good Thought came to me, asking, Who art thou? To whom dost thou belong? And I straightway answered: Zarathushtra. A foe will I be to the liar but a strong help to the righteous, that I may reach heaven. I praise and worship thee, O Mazda!

"And I knew thee as an holy one, O Mazda, when Good Thought came to me, and to my questions made answer: Ask what thou wilt; for thine asking is as that of a mighty one. . . .

"And I knew thee as an holy one, Ahura Mazda, when Good Thought came to me, and by thy words revealed the sorrow to be brought through my devotion to that which thou hast declared to be the best. Zarathushtra chooses for himself every Holy Spirit of thine."

One may think that out of the struggles of his later life, Zarathushtra realised the import of his early visions and the call to do battle for Ahura. In their lyric way the Gathic hymns of the Avesta give the accents of the story, suggesting a time in the prophet's life of gathering strength and clearing insight, of cumulative impulse becoming mastering purpose, till the man becomes the prophet. He has then not only found his god, but his god has found him, the one man amid a dumb multitude.

Ahura's spirit, Good Thought, speaks to Ahura, the supreme Lord Wisdom: "One man only have I found who will hear thy instruction and with accordant mind teach men thy law and declare the faith of Mazda."

For Zarathushtra, the false gods and all the filth and evil of the world have set themselves against the Holy Spirits of Ahura, even against that Supreme Wise Lord, Creator of righteousness and truth and all things good. The history of the world is the history of this conflict between "the world's two primal spirits, the holier one of which did thus address the evil: 'Neither do our minds, our teachings, our beliefs, our words, our deeds, or our souls agree.'" Zarathushtra's faith lifts itself into a militant dualism; but a dualism endowed with trust in the Good, and a vision which looks across the plain of battle to the final victory, at the world's end: "And I knew thee as an holy one when I beheld thee bringing to pass retribution for the wicked, reward for the good, at the world's last change, when thou, with thy holy spirit, Mazda, shalt appear with the power of Right Order and with Good Thought, through whose working men increase in Truth and Righteousness."

Direct personal trust in Mazda and the good spirits which seem his attributes or (sometimes) emanations, with fiery devotion to their cause, this is Zarathushtra's adjustment, his free will offer-

ing wherein lies the attainment of his spiritual freedom: "And Zarathushtra, he makes offering of his
life. He gives to Mazda's spirits the guidance of
his acts and words." Through defeat, through
discouragement, he will look for aid and guidance
to Ahura, to whose nature and commands he will
conform his life, and compel others so far as he may.
He is thwarted, pressed by defeat, forsaken of men:
"To what land shall I turn? Followers and kin
forsake me. How can I advance thy cause, Ahura?
I am stripped of herds and men. I cry to thee for
help; grant me support as friend to friend. Teach
me to strive for Good Thought and insight."

So Zarathushtra fights through his life, aided by
many converts, among whom is a king, Vistaspa.
We are not concerned with the subsequent fortunes
of the faith which in some way the Parsees still
hand on, which also seems to have affected later
Jewish thought and was the ancestor of Mithraism
and Manicheism. Zarathushtra's own adjustment
was not peace, but freedom to fight for the faith in
which he trusted. Even through our partial knowledge, we are impressed with the elevated spirituality
of his conceptions, with the power of his trust in
Mazda, with the energy of the thought which
marshalled in adverse camps the good and evil of
the world, and with the strength of his assurance
of lasting reward for the good, and perdition for
the wicked, at the world's final end.

CHAPTER V

THE PROPHETS OF ISRAEL

TO some extent with every people the ideals of human conduct and human life have tended to conform to their conceptions of the supreme Power or the Supreme Being. This form of the statement carries more truth than the converse one, that men have formed their ideas of God along the lines of their best thoughts of humanity. Either confusedly, as in primitive thought, or upon mature reflection, men usually have felt that the Power or Powers, good, evil, or elemental, outside themselves were different from men in nature and function. Mankind has hesitated to build up its thoughts of them wholly along conceptions of what belonged to human life or was good in human conduct. But prudential motives have always influenced men to propitiate those powers, and in some way adjust their lives to the ways or will of the divine, for the sake of their own adjustment with life and the powers of life. In fine, even if all conceptions of the divine will and nature be deemed the fruit of the human mind, nevertheless men are less apt to model them directly on the image of man than they are to conform their own lives to the likeness or the will of the Divine which they have made.

Confucius, for example, could scarcely have modelled his idea of "Heaven" and the "way of Heaven" upon man; and yet to imitate the way of Heaven was to be a sage. Neither did Lao Tzu or Chuang Tzu form the Tao on any obviously human pattern, although anxious to fashion their conduct according to its ways. In India it would likewise seem that Brahman, the Universal Absolute, was the primary, and the Atman or eternal Self the secondary and conforming concept. Both represent, however, the Indian ideal of undisturbed existence. Gotama's teachings followed the mood of the Upanishads, while revolting from their metaphysics and establishing a new psychology. But if the Absolute God and Self were dissipated, there remained a most real peace and freedom from desire, which Buddhism gradually bulwarked with eternal, more than human, Influences, to whose ways man's conduct should conform. We entered another world with Zarathushtra and his fighting God, Ahura Mazda, whom the Prophet of Iran conceived in accordance with his most strenuous ideals, and whose will he strove to carry out with a masterful devotion, paralleled only among the prophets of Israel.

We have but uncertain knowledge of the spiritual background of Israel's religion. There were elements in the religions of Chaldæa and Canaan suited to form the nucleus of her fierce tribal faith; and in Egypt waves of fluctuating monotheism were not unusual. But it was centuries after any early Egyptian associations had been severed that Israel's tribal worship broadened to the conception of Yahweh as the sole God of all the earth; while on the other hand, generally speaking, Israel's religious development advanced through strenuous disavowal both of the pressing influences of Canaan and any possible reminiscences of Chaldæa. This little book, which is not intended to be learned, may be pardoned if it turn directly to the adjustment with God reached by Israel's prophets and the most righteous of her kings.

What a picture do we have of the life-adjustment of Israel's first and apparently greatest prophet, Moses! But unhappily the earlier lines in the Pentateuch portrait are from tradition rather than from life, and have been freely painted over by later hands inspired by priestly thoughts. Each of us for himself may scan this chequered picture under the guidance of the connoisseurs who have separated layer from layer. Only we may be sure that the earlier pigments reflect in some way a man of power, whose adjustment of his life with the commands of Yahweh forecasts the train of kingly and prophetic effort to bring to pass that obedience to Yahweh's will which should draw down

prosperity betimes, but lead at last through tribulation to a larger understanding of the ways of God.

It is safer to pass on to David, where the record
is somewhat surer. Through a life of peril and
success, as a man of war and stratagem and as a
king, he is also winning his adjustment with the
power which guides and guards him. David was a
hero even in the Epic sense, combining traits of
Achilles and Odysseus. The Homeric heroes also
relied on their gods, but not with such growth of
reciprocating devotion as marks David's attitude
toward Yahweh. And yet he is less devotedly a
servant of Yahweh than the prophets, who serve
their God without regard to self. Yahweh is to
David as a father, — who can also punish: and
David, after the manner of sons, realises Yahweh's
goodness to him only in the evening of his life.
Then we see that a religious development has been
running through his life-adjustment. If he always
looked for aid to Yahweh, in the end, besides obedience, he offers in return humility and thankfulness,
devotion and desire to build Yahweh an house.
David's best acts, his righteous conduct, as when
he would not kill the sleeping Saul, had accorded
with his recognition of Yahweh's will; and the en-
noblement of his character proceeds through a larger
understanding of Yahweh's love.

The records of David's life-adjustment bear witness to the fulness of his life from the beginning,

with its eager energy and loving impulses disclosed, for instance, in those confused, but lovely,
stories of his first meeting with Saul. That his
presence, his lyre-playing, could assuage the king's
dark moods, that Saul's son and daughter loved
him, that the people sang his praises, all bespeak a
personality abounding in capacity for deeds, for
counsel, for affection, even for that outpour of
mood in song and movement which has immemorially
belonged to the heroic nature — to David, to
Achilles, or to the men of the Norse sagas.

The readiness of his genius appears in all his acts,
as when he pays the bride-price for Michal, and
then escapes from Saul's spear as well as from his
plot to murder him in bed, and concerts with
Jonathan a plan of safety. With cunning and
bravery he keeps his hunted head through his
outlawed career until made king; and no later king
in Israel was to equal his energy of rule, before the
weakness of old age came on him.

A simple faith in Yahweh quickened his courage.
It was shown in his young confidence that Yahweh
would deliver him from the paw of bear and lion
and from Goliath's spear. It pervaded and gradually beautified his life, and moulded the sense of
right and wrong so strong in him. He must keep
well with righteousness — or bitterly repent! And
righteousness with him was always that which
corresponded with Yahweh's will, while every

wrongful act was a sin against God, as it had been and ever was to be in Israel: "How can I do this great wickedness, and sin against God ?" had been Joseph's thought; and the repentant Psalmist's cry will be: "Against Thee, Thee only, have I sinned."

The incidents of David's progress in that righteousness which was identical with Yahweh's will and part of David's faith mark the course of his adjustment. He had always asked, and followed, Yahweh's counsel; and in every crisis his sense of Yahweh helped him to act righteously, as when he would not slay Yahweh's anointed who sought his life, and under other circumstances allowed himself to be turned from his revenge on the churl Nabal by the words of Abigail. A little after this, his conviction that victory and recovery of spoil are from Yahweh showed him the justice of awarding an equal share to those who kept the camp and those who went down into the battle.

The news reaches David of the flight of Israel and the death of Saul and Jonathan. Does he exult that his enemy is no more and that the crown is his ? Rather he feels the blow fallen on Yahweh's people, and with his men he mourns and fasts, while he chants that dirge:

> "Weep O Judah !
> Grieve O Israel !
> How are the mighty fallen !"

a dirge which dwells on the public calamity until the singer's grief for Jonathan presses back other thoughts:

" I am distressed for thee, my brother Jonathan: . . .
    Thy love to me was wonderful,
    Passing the love of women."

A like piety and sense of right moves him to declare before Yahweh his innocence of Abner's blood and to follow the bier in sackcloth. And it was heroic piety that moved him, pent up by war, when his mighty men had brought him water at the risk of life, to pour it out before his God.

King of all Israel, with Jerusalem taken and made the City of David, he thinks to honour Yahweh by bringing up the Ark of God. The death of the rash Uzzah frightens him for a time, till he is reassured. Then with sacrifices and the shouting of Israel, and with the king himself dancing before Yahweh with all his might, the Ark is brought up. For a great man thus to uncover himself before his maid-servants was a sheer Semitic horror — so it seemed to Michal, as she taunted him returning to his house. But David answers: "It was before Yahweh, who chose me above thy father and above all his house to appoint me prince over his people Israel — I will be more vile than this, and base in my own sight."

Then, having rest from all his enemies, David

G

plans to build Yahweh a house, as told in the seventh chapter of Second Samuel. Yahweh, by the mouth of Nathan, stays the plan, but bids the prophet tell his servant David how he took him from the sheepcote to be prince over Israel, and had been with him always, and had made him a name above the great; and now would promise him to establish his house and his seed after him in the kingdom, chastening that seed as a father, but not rejecting it. To this, David answers with full recognition of Yahweh's mercy and greatness, and begs him to make good his promise, in order that Yahweh's name may be great forever and that his servant's house may forever be established before him. "And now O Lord Yahweh, thou art God. And thy words are truth, and thou hast promised this good thing unto thy servant; now therefore let it please thee to bless the house of thy servant that it may continue forever before thee."

There follows the untoward episode of numbering the people, and the king's atoning sacrifice to stay Yahweh's mysterious wrath; then the slow incriminating story of David's crime against Uriah, and his realisation of it at the word of Nathan, and that he had sinned against Yahweh. Out of this crime and sin issues the dark and moving tale of unnatural lust, vengeance, ambition, and treachery in David's house — from which the sword should not depart! David's efficient penitence and the atonement which

lay in the growth of a contrite character were to be
evinced in the old king's acceptance of the foul
calamities coming on him and on his house from
the wickedness of the children of his loins. As the
king flees before Absalom he will not have the
priests carry forth with him the Ark of God: "Carry
back the Ark of God into the City: if I shall find
favour in the eyes of Yahweh, he will bring me
again and show me both it and his dwelling; but
if he say thus, I have no delight in thee; behold
here am I, let him do to me as seems good to him."
When Shimei curses and casts stones, the contrition
abiding in the king's heart and the sorrow that has
long been his cause him to hold back his followers:
"Behold my son which came forth from my bowels
seeks my life: how much more may this Benja-
mite? Let him alone and let him curse; for Yahweh has bidden him. It may be that Yahweh will
look on the wrong done me and will requite me good
for the cursing of this day."

In brave and faithful acts, in love of friend, in
justice, in sin, repentance, righteousness and mercy,
and through a deepening knowledge of Yahweh's
goodness, David maintained his freedom of act and
confidence of soul. In the fulness of his years,
blessing Yahweh for having given one to sit upon
his throne, his end came as the end of

> "One that ruleth over men righteously,
> That ruleth in the fear of God."

Hebrew prophecy may be included altogether under our conception of adjustment, as the harmonising of the human spirit with the powers shaping human destiny. The obvious function of the prophets was to enlighten the people, more particularly the rulers, touching the efficient nature, the commands, and the purposes of Yahweh; and to admonish them to act accordingly. The prophetic adjustment was religious, knowing no other sanction than Yahweh's will. Progressing with the enlargement of the prophetic mind, it does not represent an unchanging view of the character of the divine, but a magnificent development as the conception of Yahweh grows from age to age under the further enlightenment of experience and meditation, through which in divers ways God inspires his prophets. And one will see that the prophet's thoughts of Yahweh advance to an emphatic and, one may say, international monotheism, through observation of Yahweh's power fashioning the fate of Israel and the destinies of nations, and operative within the heart of man. In like manner, Zarathushtra's thought of Ahura Mazda sprang forward from exigency to exigency, pragmatically as it were, and not through ontological meditations on the divine nature, such as arose in India.

So the adjustment which the prophets demanded of Yahweh's people was moulded, and continually remoulded, on those enlarging thoughts of Yahweh's

will and purposes with which succeeding prophets
were inspired. The untowardness of events was a
stumbling-block and then again a goad, driving the
prophets on to the attainment of conceptions constantly uplifting. Never did the remnant of a
people so wrestle with God for an adjustment of
their minds with the course of their destinies and
the power controlling them, as did the larger minded
Jews, crushed beneath the shock of Syrian and Assyrian, of Babylonian, Persian, Greek.

The prophetic adjustment drives, or is driven, on.
With respect to thoughts of God, it wins its way from
Yahweh as the peremptory god of Israel, to Yahweh
as the sole and only god, supreme in the power of
his righteousness over all nations; and with respect
to thoughts of man, of Israel, it wins its way through
the spent hopes of national prosperity, the conviction of common sin and a people's responsibility,
to the thought of each individual's guilt or innocence; whereupon it seems incited to discriminate
obscurely between the lots of the righteous and
the wicked beyond the grave; but with the ineradi-
cable tribal consciousness of the Jew, it turns more
surely to the thought of a national adjustment
thrown forward to some future time, and harbouring
within the walls of a triumphant New Jerusalem,
which is sanctified through Yahweh's presence; or
the prophetic thought bows down sublimely before
an ideal of Israel as Yahweh's servant, afflicted and

redeemed in the service of his other children on the earth.

In the careers of the prophets there is none of Jacob's patriarchal egotism or David's royal fore-handedness. They are Yahweh's spokesmen. As for their personal adjustment, that may appear in the light of their exhortations to others. Moreover, since Israel was one people, bound together through blood, as well as through Yahweh's covenant made with them as a people, the personal adjustment of the prophets was merged in this common solidarity. Did not that include Yahweh, of whom it was declared, "In all the affliction of his people he is afflicted"? Likewise his prophets were afflicted in the affliction of his people and blessed in their prosperity. But we may think that a prophet's surest stay was the sense that he was Yahweh's servant, admitted to his confidences, and to a knowledge of his will and purposes: "Surely Yahweh does nothing unless he reveals his secrets to his servants the prophets."

Elijah's understanding of Yahweh's will affords an opening illustration of the prophetic adjustment. Ahab is king of northern Israel; he has married the Sidonian princess Jezebel, has led his people to worship Baal, and sorely persecuted the prophets of Yahweh. Elijah has to his face foretold his punishment through a consuming drought upon the land; and when the drought is in its third year, he again confronts Ahab with the challenge to determine whether Baal or Yahweh be God — for Elijah's Yahweh will tolerate no other god or idol in his land. When the king has gathered all Israel unto Mount Carmel, Elijah demands of the people, "How long halt ye between two opinions: if Yahweh be God, follow him, if the Baal, then follow him." And after the test is ended, and Yahweh's fire has consumed the burnt offering and the altar, there comes the word, "Take the prophets of the Baal, let not one of them escape."

Yahweh will endure no other god in Israel — this conviction is one phase of Elijah's adjustment. The other is his realisation of Yahweh's justice, so fiercely to be vindicated upon Ahab and Jezebel for the crime of Naboth murdered for his vineyard: "In the place where dogs licked the blood of Naboth, shall dogs lick thy blood." But in the meanwhile, even after his triumph on Mount Carmel, flying from Jezebel, a very queenly woman, Elijah in the cave on Horeb, has known the earthquake and the tempest there; and after them, in the contrasted quiet, he has heard Yahweh's still small voice directing him.

Elijah's mantle fell on Elisha, who seems his master's replica, but with his story set in rather questionable miracles. It is not clear that he advanced the thought of God. So we pass on to Amos, the earliest prophet whose writings, or at least utterances, survive. Since Elijah's death a hundred years had passed. Now the prophetic vision had need to embrace not only the small rival peoples surrounding the kingdoms of northern Israel and Judah, but beyond them the powerful Damascus, and Assyria impending from afar. The vision of Amos has thus widened, with the result that he knows Yahweh as the just god of all these nations, and not of Israel alone. Very penetrating was the vision of Amos; if he came from among the shepherds of the village of Tekoa, his knowledge of life could scarcely have been gained within their circle.

Seemingly Israel, the northern kingdom to which Amos spoke, was then prospering. He saw the idolatry practised there, and the injustice and oppression which prevailed — prevailed at least for the stern eye whose business was to see evil. This eye also saw Israel as a people, and foresaw the punishment which was to come upon that people, and make no distinction between individuals. His vision did not extend beyond the present life to discern the discriminating awards of a life beyond the grave. But if the judges of the people would hate evil and love good, and establish justice in the gate, perhaps the God of hosts would still be gracious to a remnant of Joseph.[1] Then would come firm na-

[1] Amos v. 15. Joseph here means Israel in the sense of the northern kingdom, exclusive of Judah. One applies the name

tional well-being, in which the fortunes of obedient Israel would be adjusted with Yahweh's beneficent disposition toward his people. *His* people indeed! there was the pivot of the difference between Amos and the moral blind in Israel. They looked on Yahweh as their partisan, their god to help and keep them; Amos also knew that they were Yahweh's people, led by Him and known of Him; but for that very reason Yahweh's justice must visit on them all their iniquities. A sad reversal here of the view so naturally popular! The people looked foward to the "day of Yahweh," as a day of triumph! They would find it darkness.

To give point to his denunciations, Amos set forth Yahweh as a righteous god, impartial and of universal power, creator of the world: "It is he that maketh the stars; who formeth the mountains and createth wind, and declareth his thought to man; maketh sunrise and darkness and marcheth over the heights of the earth; and his name is Yahweh the god of hosts.

"He toucheth the earth and it melts, and all who dwell in it mourn, and it shall rise up wholly and sink like the River of Egypt. He it is who buildeth his chambers in the heaven and foundeth his vault upon the earth.

Israel to all the tribes, and then again to the northern kingdom, separated from Judah after the death of Solomon. The words "Ephraim" and "Samaria" apply to the northern region.

"Are ye not as the sons of the Cushites to me, ye sons of Israel, — saith Yahweh. Did I not lead up Israel from Egypt, and the Philistines from Caphtor, and the Syrians from Kir ? Behold, the eyes of Yahweh are upon the sinful kingdom, and I will destroy it from the face of the earth, only I will not utterly destroy the house of Jacob."

Harsh indeed the message of Amos. His younger contemporary Hosea softens it through telling of the clinging love of Yahweh, which will not willingly cast off — nay which will draw Israel back to her god, if only that may be ! — "When Israel was young, I loved him, and out of Egypt called my son hither. So much the further have they gone astray ; to Baal they sacrifice, and burn incense to graven images. Yet I taught Ephraim to walk, held him by his arms." The prophet knows that the sword must consume Ephraim's iniquity, yet he hears Yahweh's voice crying, "Oh ! how shall I give thee up, Ephraim ? abandon thee, Israel ? Oh, how shall I treat thee as Adma, make thee as Zeboim ? Mine heart is turned within me. I will not execute the heat of mine anger, will not destroy Ephraim ; for I am God, and not man ; Holy in thy midst."

Israel was as a silly dove, running to and fro, looking for aid now to Egypt, now to Assyria. All foolish wickedness — from the prophetic point of view. Yahweh will have Israel trust him altogether. And his love, the prophet declares, is ready to attach itself anew to Israel's repentance. "Return, O Israel, unto Yahweh thy God! For you have stumbled with your guilt. Take with you words of penitence, return and say to Yahweh, 'Forgive all guilt, and accept what is good. We will offer our repentant lips instead of bullocks. Assyria shall not save us, [Egypt's] horses we will not ride, nor any more call the work of our hands our god.' 'I will heal their falling away, gladly love them; for mine anger is turned away. I will be as dew unto Israel; he shall blossom as the lily, and thrust forth his roots as Lebanon.'"

Yahweh is god universal; the other gods are nought. Hosea says it clearly: "Samaria's calf! a workman made it, and it is no god." This is monotheism, though its scope may be extended with riper experience. Hosea's forecasting spirit seems to waver: by the visible evil and approaching danger, he is drawn to prophesy destruction; yet Yahweh's saving love endures — if only the people will repent!

The mind of Hosea, like the mind of Amos, and in general, the mind of the Old Testament prior to the Exile, dwells in the conviction that obedience to the righteous will of Yahweh will establish Israel in safety and gladness. The righteous prosper, — that is a basic conviction. The prophetic adjustment still abides in this assurance; it has not yet taken refuge in the hope of a future Israel redeemed

and reëstablished in obedient communion with
Yahweh, forever in their midst. Still less has there
come the thought of a recompense for the down-
trodden righteous in the resurrection of the dead.
Life for these earlier prophets is altogether in the
body, though its best part be a communing
with Yahweh. He upholds his people in their
homes, in their comings and goings, their flock-
raisings and godly businesses throughout their land,
and will uphold them so long as they obey, or for
his love's sake, perhaps a little longer. But Amos
and Hosea see disobedience throughout the northern
kingdom and foresee the ruin coming as its consequence from Assyria. That also will be Yahweh's
act.

One doubts the validity of the one horn or the
other of the prophetic thesis. Israel herself was to
learn that the righteous may not prosper, and that
the ungodly often prosper obviously. In these respects the prophetic adjustment does not satisfy;
although the prophets in their assurance of Yahweh,
their god, who rules all nations in the power of his
righteousness, have established what will prove
valid for ages.

Younger than Hosea and Amos, the Judean Isaiah
lived to see the northern kingdom fall, and a like
ruin threaten his own Jerusalem. Gifted of Yahweh
beyond other men, and taught by what he saw and
foresaw, it was his lot to test the prophetic adjust-

ment already reached, invest it with new glories of imagery and new power of expression, qualify and amplify it through further consideration of its conclusions in the light of his knowledge of Yahweh and experience of disasters coming upon men; and then deepen and enlarge it through the power of his genius. Isaiah's name is hallowed, not only through the utterances which were his, but also by reason of those ascribed to him, to which have clung the hopes of men. But it is difficult, in the changing lights of modern criticism, to decide which portions of the first thirty-nine chapters of the great prophetic book should be ascribed to this Judæan, whose eyes were stricken with the sight of present evil, and calamities approaching, in the second half of the eighth century before Christ.

Isaiah's convictions as to the character and commands of Yahweh may be said to combine those of Amos and Hosea. Only in him monotheism is deepened and illuminated. He saw more clearly than his elders that the nations were but Yahweh's instruments, rods of his anger, the axes with which God hews ; and with scornful clarity he showed the folly of presenting in expiation before Yahweh anything but faith and righteousness. Reliance on heathen aid — upon Egypt — is madness. Faith in Yahweh, joined with right conduct and freedom from idolatries of thought and act, are the horsemen and the chariots of Judah. Righteousness and national well-being go together, are bone of each other's bone, flesh of each other's flesh; they are included and assured in obedience and faith.

How could Isaiah doubt of this, knowing Yahweh to be righteous and all-powerful and Israel's god, who held Israel as sons reared by him, — how could he doubt but that Judah would prosper if obedient, established in the land which Yahweh had given to his people? But Judah's actual state drives this assurance from his mind, which perforce is filled with realisation of the suicidal disobedience and folly of rulers and people, their empty rites and no-gods, their sought-for pleasant answers and wilful falsities of hope and policy, — sin added to sin, bringing destruction. Hence most of the prophet's utterances are warnings and denunciations and predictions of ruin, now falling on Israel, soon to fall on Judah, finally to fall upon that rod of Yahweh's wrath, Assyria.

Is Isaiah moved, a little in the manner of those who afterwards wrote marvels in his name, to push forward his hopes, beyond the horizon of the present, to some assurance of future restoration or individual blessedness? He possessed that most unshaken of Old Testament convictions, that of Yahweh's faith-keeping with his people, his mercy and benevolence, and his saving purpose. Yahweh had no more delight in Israel's disasters than in the sins of which they were the result: he did not

willingly afflict or grieve his people. But in those
closing decades of the eighth century, a man with
Isaiah's mind could not but foresee the probable
realisation of his conditional prediction, the down-
fall of Judah as well as of that northern kingdom,
which fell before he had ceased from prophesying.
If he expected Judah's fall, must he not modify his
hopes, his convictions regarding Israel, in fine his
adjustment, in order to hold fast to his assurance of
Yahweh's love and mercy ? Did it come to him to
project this assurance into the future, and behold in
certain hope a restoration, a redemption of a people
now staggering to ruin ? Was it given only to some
later seer, or did Isaiah foresee the time when
the people who walked in darkness should behold
a great light, when the yoke of Israel should be
broken, and a child should have been born upon
whose shoulder dominion shall rest ? who shall
be the Prince of Peace upon the throne of David,
and to whose kingdom there shall be no end ? A
time when a king shall reign righteously, and princes
rule justly, like water courses in a parched land and
the shadow of a high rock ! When the folly of the
fool and the knavery of the knave shall be laid bare;
but the eyes of them that see shall not be dim and
the ears of them that hear shall hearken, and the
stammerer's tongue speak plain ? [1]

---

[1] Isaiah ix. 1–7; xxxii. 1–8.

If this vision was not Isaiah's, his refuge still was Yahweh's righteousness to be shown in the chastening, perhaps in the necessary destruction of his people; for Isaiah did not advance to a discrimination between the righteous Israelites who should be saved and the wicked who should perish. That progress in the prophetic adjustment was left to Jeremiah and Ezekiel, — and perhaps to the Book of Deuteronomy.

The book last named may have been written not very long before the year of Jeremiah's call (626 B.C.) and was "found" by Hilkiah the high priest in the temple in the eighteenth year of Josiah's reign (621 B.C.). Its burden was the Covenant between Yahweh and his people; and its exhortation was to keep from graven images, from heathenism, and wickedness, to fear Yahweh, and walk in all his ways, and keep his statutes, and love and serve him alone with entire heart and soul and strength; so would Yahweh fulfil the Covenant which he swore unto their Father Abraham, and unto them at Horeb when he commanded them to keep his statutes; then he would make his people blessed and numerous as the stars, in the land which he had promised unto Abraham. But their covenant to obey did not lie in outer acts alone; they should circumcise the foreskin of their heart. And although the time-honoured thought of visiting the sins of the fathers upon the children is retained as of course in the Deuteronomic decalogue, nevertheless in that book Yahweh's statutes are brought home to every Israelite, making him individually responsible for his acts: "The fathers shall not be put to death for the children, neither shall the children be put to death for the fathers, every man shall be put to death for his own sin." [1] Thus the book seems to set before each man, as well as before the nation, life and death, the blessing and the curse, that the people and every one of them may choose life, to love Yahweh and cleave to him, as their life and length of days, so that they may dwell in the land promised to their fathers.

Composed during the flickerings out of kingship in Judah, Deuteronomy still earnestly treats the people as a nation, still exhorts them to the perfected fulfilment of Yahweh's statutes, and to the final obedience of love. And the king, Josiah, undertook a reform and purification of his kingdom according to the mandates of this new-found book.[2] But the end could not be averted. Josiah was but a child when he began to reign, and to reward his youthful reforming righteousness, Yahweh held back the ruin of his kingdom for the little while until he should sleep with his fathers. The prophetic work of Jeremiah began in the thirteenth year of Josiah; it continued forty years, through the

---

[1] Deut. xxiv. 16. See Deut. v. 9, and Ex. xx. 5 and xxxiv. 7.
[2] 2 Kings xxii. and xxiii.

H

foolish reigns of the last kinglets. He saw the first
siege of Jerusalem and the carrying into exile of its
better part (597 B.C.); and eleven years later the final
destruction of the city by the Chaldæans. Judging
from the general tone of Jeremiah's admonitions, the
reforms of Josiah had but scratched the surface of
Judah's guilt; perhaps they had helped to blow up
the false hope that an observance of ritual would
ward off the Babylonian attack.

Jeremiah was not born in the city, but in a village
a few miles to the north. One may think of him as
a young, well-nurtured countryman abruptly struck
with the luxury and corruption of the capital; and
yet he was not more impressed by it than the highborn and city-bred Isaiah had been before him.
This country youth, in spite of his bashful sense of
his own ineptitude, knows that he is chosen, even
before he came forth from the womb, to be a "brazen
wall against the kings of Judah, the princes and the
common people."

It is largely the old, old story of denunciation
of idolatry, luxury, wickedness — of so much that
made the common round of life in town and country.
Such admonitions reached their final Cassandra stri-
dency in the utterances of this man who realised
the shifty folly of Judean politics and foresaw their
consequences. And yet how could a little crumbling
state do otherwise than turn from one to another of
its dominant neighbours, according to the apparent

shifting of power ?   The affairs of western Asia and
Egypt were in a flux as the seventh century ended
and the sixth began — when Scythians had made
breaches in the Assyrian empire, and the Medes
had entered therein; when Babylon had risen to
the south, strong and independent, and a dynastic
revolution had made Egypt for the time aggressive,
yet had not given her the strength to stand against
the arms of Babylon.

The emotional and one might say overwrought
utterances of this prophet have sustained the tradition of a man of contention and lament, who was
wont to curse the day of his birth, because of the
burden of his life and his prophetic office; who
frequently besought Yahweh to avenge him of his
enemies, — deliver over their children to famine,
their young men to the sword, their wives to widow-
hood.   He was beset with danger and contumely,
mobbed in his own village, in the capital cast into a
putrid cistern, again imprisoned, threatened with
death; all of which quite naturally was put upon one
who would prophesy nothing but evil, and appeared
in Jerusalem's streets with a yoke upon his neck to
signify the yoke which Nebuchadnezzar would set
on the neck of Judah.   In the end when the last
weak king had rebelled against the overlord to whom
he had pledged his fealty, Jeremiah advised men to
escape from the city and seek safety in the Chaldæan
camp.   He himself attempted to go out, but was

arrested at the gate. Surely some fear of Yahweh
must have lain on king and princes, that they did
not kill such a grievously clear-seeing man!

How could Jeremiah cherish any present hope of
the people of Judah? Weeping, he had implored
Yahweh, and Yahweh had answered that though
Moses and Samuel should plead for them, yet
would he cast them forth (Jer. xv. 1). So, foreseeing their destruction as a nation, and the destruction of that symbol of nationality, the Temple,
Jeremiah reached the conception of a further adjustment. His faith discriminates; let the wicked
perish and the righteous live. If Yahweh indeed
was known as a god to "recompense the iniquity
of the fathers into the bosoms of the children,"
still would not the time come when it should no
more be said that the fathers have eaten sour grapes
and the children's teeth are set on edge? when,
rather, every man should die for his own iniquity?
But then would not Yahweh's covenant be broken?
— at least, how could its counter-conditions be fulfilled by a nation which was to be destroyed before
the prophet's eyes? Jeremiah's conception, if it still
remained national, became spiritual; and he found
his grand adjustment in a new covenant between
Yahweh and the House of Israel, not like the
covenant made with their fathers when he brought
them out of the land of Egypt — which they broke:

"But this is the covenant that I will make with

the House of Israel, after those days, says Yahweh.
I will put my law in their breast, and write it in
their hearts, and I will be their God and they shall
be my people. And they shall teach no more
every man his neighbour and every man his brother,
saying, Know Yahweh, for they shall all know me,
from the least of them to the greatest of them, says
Yahweh; for I will forgive their iniquity and I will
remember their sin no more."

This new Covenant is with the House of Israel.
But it is written on the heart of every Israelite,
and not on tablets of stone set in a public place.
Can we say that the House of Israel consists of those
in whose hearts this righteousness is written, rather
than of those who are born Israelites? Or shall it
be that all who are of that stock in those days will
be righteous? Jeremiah looked forward certainly
to Israel's restoration, and symbolised his assurance
by purchasing his uncle's field, and putting the deed
away to remain for years to come, when, as Yahweh
said, Houses and fields and vineyards should be
possessed again in the land. His book has proph-
ecies of future restoration. Some of them may
not have been uttered by this man who saw Judah's
ruin and the carrying away of her sons. But as he
heard the voice in Ramah of Rachel weeping for
her children and refusing to be comforted, so he
also heard Yahweh bidding him cry: Refrain thy
voice from weeping and thine eyes from tears;

for they shall come again from the land of the enemy, and thy children shall return — Ephraim as well as Judah.

There is a noble consideration of the ways of God in the third poem of that book of Dirges so long ascribed to Jeremiah, and composed after the city's fall. Yahweh's hand has been heavy on the speaker and on Judah, but his soul chants, — "it is of Yahweh's mercies that we are not utterly consumed, because his compassions fail not. They are new every morning: great is thy faithfulness. Yahweh is my portion, saith my soul; therefore will I hope in him. . . . It is good that a man should both hope and quietly wait on the salvation of Yahweh. . . . For Yahweh will not cast off forever . . . for he doth not afflict willingly nor grieve the children of men. . . . Let us search and try our ways and turn again to Yahweh. . . . Mine eye runneth down with rivers of water for the destruction of the daughter of my people. . . . I called upon thy name, O Yahweh, out of the low dungeon. Thou heardest my voice. . . . O Yahweh, thou hast pleaded the causes of my soul; thou hast redeemed my life."

Was any people ever so spiritually quickened by tribulation as the Jews? They reached their highest thoughts of God, of *their* god, Yahweh, only when he had cast them down in exile. It was then that they conceived more clearly the duties of their fealty and the privileges of their hope in him. They realised not only his sole sovereignty over all the peoples of the earth, but also his purpose, in that they were to be his people not for themselves alone, but for the glory of his name and as a light to the nations. Ezekiel, the priest prophet, and the great unnamed ones whose utterances make part of the Book of Isaiah, present these latter stages of the prophetic adjustment, the last before prophecy became what is called apocalyptic.

The idea of individual responsibility is set forth in Ezekiel's eighteenth chapter: "Behold all souls are mine; as the soul of the father, so also the soul of the son is mine: the soul that sinneth, it shall die. . . . The son shall not bear the iniquity of the father, neither shall the father bear the iniquity of the son: the righteousness of the righteous shall be upon him, and the wickedness of the wicked shall be upon him. But if the wicked will turn from all his sins that he has committed, and keep all my statutes, and do that which is lawful and right, he shall surely live, he shall not die. . . . Have I any pleasure in the death of the wicked? . . . But when a righteous man turneth away from his righteousness, and committeth iniquity, he shall die." Ezekiel's own righteousness was to be that of a watchman to the House of Israel, to warn the wicked man from his way — and if he turn not from his wickedness, he shall die: but thou hast saved thyself.[1]

[1] Cf. Ez. iii. 16–21; xiv. 9–20; xxxiii. 1–9.

Thus explicitly, with more emphasis than clarity, the principle of individual responsibility thrusts itself to the front of Ezekiel's adjustment. Yet his interest still centres in Israel as a people; as is evident in the promises which follow of future restoration when Yahweh shall make a covenant of peace with his ill-shepherded flock, and set over them my servant David. The tenor of this restoration, with its forgiveness and its spiritual regeneration, are set forth: "Son of man, when the house of Israel dwelt in their own land, they defiled it by their ways and doings . . . wherefore I poured out my fury upon them . . . and I scattered them among the nations. And when they came among the nations, they profaned my holy name. . . . Therefore say unto the house of Israel, I do not this for your sake, O house of Israel, but for my holy name, which ye have profaned among the nations whither ye have gone. And I will sanctify my great name . . . which ye have profaned, and the nations shall know that I am Yahweh. . . . For I will take you from the nations, and gather you out of all countries, and will bring you into your own land. And I will sprinkle clean water upon you, and ye shall be clean. . . . A new heart also will I give you, and a new spirit will I put within you. . . . And I will put my spirit within you, and cause you to walk in my statutes, and ye shall keep my judgements, and do them. And ye shall dwell

in the land that I gave to your fathers; and ye
shall be my people, and I will be your God. . . .
Then shall ye remember your evil ways . . . and
ye shall loath yourselves in your own sight for your
iniquities and abominations" (Ez. xxxvi.).

The vision of the valley of dry bones reclothed
with flesh symbolises the character of the restoration
— the dry bones both of (northern) Israel and Judah
shall be made one nation in the land, under one king.
Then Yahweh's victory shall follow over the nations
who assault his people. After this comes the building of that temple, so elaborately described, in which
Yahweh shall forever dwell, in his people's midst.

In Ezekiel's closed and priestly mind, this restoration is of the people of Israel; and the Temple is
for their god, exclusively for him and them. The
nations have no share. Yahweh's service is purified
from every gentile taint, even from lay participation,
and is confided to the holy priesthood; his ritual
becomes as strict as the statutory righteousness which
he demands of his people. Ezekiel's adjustment
was formal and for Israel alone; and his ideals were
to dominate the legalistic phases of later Judaism.
But others spoke more universal hopes, and other
minds than that of this priest-prophet applied
themselves to the mystery of the connexion between
righteousness or sin and the prosperity or misery of
the righteous or sinning individual or people. From
the period of the exile, the Old Testament writings

may be regarded as a literature of adjustment of the facts and hopes of Israel, of the Israelites, of universal man, with the power and the steadfastly assumed righteousness of God.

It is difficult not to regard the Exile as providential. Who has not realised how in some way he, or she, has learned through tribulation ? From suffering, wisdom, said Æschylus. Israel furnishes national illustration of the theme. For centuries they had felt themselves a people, delivered and preserved through the power of their righteous god, whose special care they were; he had established them for ever in the land which he had covenanted to them. Now this people, and, more especially, that better part which most keenly felt itself Israel, had been taken from their heritage to labour as a captive community in the midst of their overweening enemies. It was for them to brood upon their lot as a people collectively chastened, punished, cast out by their god, — for a time ? forever ? with what intent ?—or they might muse upon God's treatment of the individual, the good or wicked man. How was Israel to be repaired, restored again, in some conformity with these exiles' unshakable conviction of Yahweh's power and righteousness and peculiar care of his people ? And, considering like matters less nationally, more particularly, how reconcile God's justice with the divers lots of men ? and having regard to this more individual adjustment, how teach man to conduct his life ? Struggling for the solution of these problems, certain Israelites, either of the Exile or still dwelling in an orphaned land, reached the sublimest expression of their faith in Yahweh's righteousness and love. Their solutions did not rest on human wisdom and energy. Yahweh did all, inspired the thoughts of men, fulfilled or frustrated them, and brought to pass the destinies of nations.

With the fall of Jerusalem and the extinction of every ray of present national hope, those whose minds clung to the destinies of Israel were forced to look far into the future and draw their peace from thoughts of redemption and restoration. It was partly thus with Jeremiah and wholly thus with Ezekiel. And when Jerusalem's fall brought further bands of exiles to Babylon, the nation of Israel seemed broken into small communities settled in the midst of alien multitudes. The restoration of such bands to national integrity and territorial power in far-off Judea gradually lost material likelihood. Yahweh could accomplish even this; but his purposes were clothed with the majesty of righteousness. Israel's restoration must be such as to exemplify the character, sublime and spiritual, of the god of all the earth. Evidently Yahweh's purpose, as his power, was of world-wide scope. It would not simply restore Israel to what she was before : her restoration must be an incident, a means for the accomplishment of Yahweh's universal plan of righteousness. In consonance with these necessities of thought, the idealising prophets of the Exile raised and sanctified their conceptions of Israel's restoration and final destinies.

It were futile to set forth the adjustments of Israel's destinies with Yahweh's character and purposes as conceived in the exilic portions of the Book of Isaiah, save in those words and images which have compelled men's imaginations and spoken their most sacred hopes for the last two thousand years. The imagery clothing the thought and feeling of these writings has lent itself to the plastic conceptions of successive and diverse generations. Representing the highest truth of poetic expression, it does not gain in clarity by analytic restatement. Yet we may recall the background of these utterances. In certain chapters of the first part of Isaiah (whether he be their author, or another) Yahweh works his purpose with a redeemed and sanctified Israel, through a king of David's line whose righteousness is Yahweh's righteousness, and whose power is Yahweh's power.[1] Unto him shall the nations seek. This idea was natural before David's house had fallen utterly, and it continued long afterwards to move men in whom the memory of that house was strong. Yet as one decade of servitude succeeded another, and

[1] Is. ix., xi., xxxii.   Cf. the much disputed Zech. ix.

the hope of a royal embodiment of Yahweh's rule
waned with the exiles, it was replaced by a counter-
thought of profounder religious content.   Righteous
kings, prophets, and priests had held themselves
and the people also to be Yahweh's servants.   As
their religion rose to the thought of one righteous
God of all the earth, the conception of their service
rose in correspondence. Serving Yahweh meant
serving his design of world-wide redemption.   In
Babylon, Jews were not kings, but servants : the
visible servitude of their condition might suggest
new aspects of their destiny and mission. If
Israel was to be redeemed and restored, might it
not be in the rôle of Yahweh's servant, at a time
when Yahweh's name should be honoured throughout
the earth ?

In many ways thoughts of peace and blessedness,
springing from free responsive service, would touch
devoted minds, whose conviction of Yahweh's
righteousness had never faltered. A service of
universal mediation was disclosed; and thoughts
came of atonement through suffering, atonement
for Israel and for the sinful nations; then an assurance of forgiveness, of redemption and restoration
within the scope of Yahweh's purposes, and of final
peace and comforting through Yahweh's presence
in a redeemed Israel.   Service and atonement would
be sanctified in blessedness, and rewarded with
pre-eminence among the nations.

A very marvellous adjustment, or series of adjustments, is unfolded by the prophet, or prophets, of the last twenty-seven chapters of the Book of Isaiah. It is an adjustment with God, and is brought to pass through Yahweh's forgiveness, his redeeming love, and the power of his spirit moving the destinies of men, and acting within their hearts. Israel (not as the prophet knows her to be, but as he dreamed of her) acts and suffers in obedience and responsive love. It is Yahweh who redeems her surely, and compels the nations to his ends. Yahweh omnipotent in the world, the sole power that accomplishes; also resistless in the heart, wakening its ear morning by morning. He bruises his servant, makes him one to bear men's sicknesses, and the sin of many, and lay down his soul an offering for guilt. In his service the Servant is very close to Yahweh, who had been afflicted in all the afflictions of his people, had cried out like a woman in travail, and had drawn into his passionate redemptive purpose this Servant, in order to make many righteous, and thereby make redemption possible for Israel and the nations. The willingness to suffer! the Servant has this in common with his God. As he has been bruised and his visage marred, so from the travail of his soul shall he also be satisfied, when there shall be proclaimed "an acceptable year of Yahweh, and a day of vengeance of our God; to comfort the mournful ones of Zion, to give them oil of joy for the raiment of mourning. . . . And they shall build up the ruins of old, and renew the wasted cities. . . . And strangers shall stand and feed your flocks, shall be your ploughmen and vine-dressers; but ye, priests of Yahweh shall ye be called; men shall name you the messengers of our God; ye shall eat the riches of the nations and make your boast of their glory."

Tumultuous words these, and many more: vengeance on the oppressor, restoration, triumph, and priestly mediation to the nations, of whose riches the redeemed shall eat. Tumultuous thoughts! The vision of Yahweh overcomes at last: "Hark thy watchmen! They lift up their voice: they cry together, for they see eye to eye the return of Yahweh to Zion." Threats and promises mingle to the end of the prophecy, and world-wide mediation follows upon Israel's victory, through her god, over her enemies. But the wicked ones of Israel shall also be cut off, and not impede the salvation of the faithful. "I will create a new heaven and a new earth . . . and I will exult in Jerusalem and rejoice in my people." Rites and sacrifices shall be nothing. "Thus saith Yahweh: Heaven is my throne, and the earth is my footstool; what manner of house would ye build me? and where is the place of my habitation? All these my hand has made, and all these are mine. But I have regard for him that is of a poor and contrite spirit, and trembles at my

word." Tumultuous words! But the infinity and
spirituality of God pierces through them, and the
comfort of the Servant's presence with his god.

It is still the redemption of the nation that is
borne in mind, though its chaff will be sifted from its
wheat. The prophet who is speaking is very near
to Yahweh, folded in the assurance of his presence.
Likewise the Servant, whether that Servant be an
individual or an ideal Israel. This intimate assurance is the stronghold of his peace and freedom. His
also is that holding close to God, that passionate
adjustment which fills the Psalter and makes it the
supplement and completion of the exhortations and
the warnings of the prophets, — an adjustment held
in religious feeling, and resting on the assurance of
God and the sense that man's vital relationship with
God is sufficient for him. Since He moves and
surely governs all, and holds man in His hand,
even to His heart, making man to be part of the
divine purpose and event, then come what may,
welfare or misery, life or death, nothing can divide
man from the rock of his salvation, the living God.

The Psalms set forth God's greatness, righteousness, spirituality, his compassion and loving-kindness. But their veritable theme is the consciousness
of man before his God. The emotions of the Psalmist
may be occasioned by the incidents of human lots;
but they spring from man's realisation of the over-
whelming relationship of God to man. The Psalms

express the Israelite's sense of self before Yahweh, —
a sense of shortcoming, but sometimes of integrity;
a sense of littleness before Yahweh's grandeur, of
impotence beneath Yahweh's power, of awe before
Yahweh's works: and then a sense of the desolation
which is severance from God. There presses to
utterance the fear of Yahweh, love of Yahweh, zeal
and jealousy for him, and yearning for his presence:
with these come repentance and turning from sin, a
longing to be pure in Yahweh's sight, and to be
forgiven; a longing for God's love, even for His
sympathy. Thus the nature of man in its whole
compass, sets as the tide toward God, to be met by
the flooding sense of God's loving-kindness and the
majesty of his ways. Any feeling of the untoward
lot of the Psalmist is blotted out.

How shall Yahweh not be enough for man?

"O Yahweh, thou hast searched me and known me;
    Thou knowest my downsitting and my uprising,
    Thou understandest my thought afar off.
        .   .   .   .

"Such knowledge is too wonderful for me,
    It is too high, I cannot attain unto it.
    Whither shall I go from thy spirit ?
    Or whither shall I flee from thy presence ?
    If I climb up into heaven, thou art there,
    If I take the wings of the morning,
    If I dwell in the uttermost parts of the sea,
    Even there shall thy hand lead me,
    And thy right hand shall hold me.
        .   .   .   .

I

"And how precious unto me are thy thoughts, O God!
How great is the sum of them!
If I would tell them they are more in number than the
sands;
When I awake, I am still with thee."

Truly can the Psalmist exclaim: Thy loving-
kindness is better than life; and can realise how
God's love covers all: Thou makest the outgoings of
the morning to sing for joy. And as for life's
hard phases:

"Fret not thyself because of evil-doers!
Hold thee still for Yahweh, and hope in him."

Yahweh's sufficiency, — to abide in that is the life
of the righteous: and what part have the wicked in
the felt presence of the living God?

"Like as a hart which panteth after the water-brooks,
So panteth my soul after thee, O God."

The Psalter has also its depths of woe: My God,
my God! why has thou forsaken me? The *melan-
cholia*, the depression when man feels forsaken of God,
this is the Psalmist's grief, which crushes other woes.
Beneath it, his thoughts seem to break in sorrow,
and suggest a bitter lack of the assurance of a life
beyond the grave. It would seem so in the eighty-
eighth psalm.

"O Yahweh, God of my salvation,
I have cried day and night before thee.
Let my prayer come before thee,

Incline thine ear to my cry.
For my soul is full of troubles,
And my life draweth near unto the grave.
I am counted with them that go down into the pit,

. . . .

"Whom thou rememberest no more.

. . . .

Wilt thou shew wonders to the dead?
Shall the dead arise and praise thee?
Shall thy loving-kindness be told in the grave?

. . . .

"And thy righteousness in the land of forgetfulness?

. . . .

"Why, O Yahweh, casteth thou off my soul?"

Yet even without this further hope, the Psalmist,
save in black moments, conquers through his faith,
which is a realisation of Yahweh — and of man.
That is the Psalmist's adjustment. But a lack of
this assurance keeps the Book of Job from presenting
an adjustment for souls torn by the question, why
does the righteous man suffer? The Book remains,
in the eye of reason, a majestic statement of the
problem. Yet in Job, as in the Psalms, if Yahweh's
majesty does not satisfy the sufferer's longings, it
overwhelms his mind and closes his mouth.

Stung by the ruthless one-sided arguments of the
friends, Job flings himself upon his thought of God,
his determination to be justified by Him, — if not
now, hereafter. From beneath the surges of his
afflictions, the thought of God in His infinite works

lifts the sufferer above his doubts of God's righteousness :

"Lo, these are but the outskirts of his ways,
And how small a whisper do we hear of him !
But the thunder of his power, who can understand ?"

Job is confident that, though the righteous may suffer, it is not well with the wicked, whose cry shall surely be unheard of Him who decrees that for man the fear of Yahweh is wisdom, and to depart from evil is understanding. That furthest wisdom, which is Yahweh's plan and understanding, is His alone. The sufferer is mastered by his yearning for restored communion : he is ready for that vision of power which is Yahweh's answer from the whirlwind. Man, dost thou know, dost thou possess, anything wherewith to plumb the ways of God ? "Now that mine eyes have seen thee," is Job's answer, "I abhor myself and repent in dust and ashes."

Such is Job's adjustment — though the Hebrew sense of fitness insisted that the book should end with Yahweh's giving Job "twice as much as he had before." [1]

Unavoidably the prophetic adjustment or situation, the adjustment in the Psalms, and the crushing answer to Job's problem, all moved together toward

[1] In its practical gnomic way the teaching of the Book of Proverbs parallels the argumentation of the Book of Job.

the completion which one and all implicitly demanded, that is to say toward the supplementing of
earthly life with a life beyond the grave. This
aspiration dawns through Job's agonies, and here
and there touches the surface in the Psalter. In the
nineteenth verse of the twenty-sixth chapter of
Isaiah, written in the fourth or fifth century before
Christ, the resurrection of the dead is plainly stated,
and more elaborately in the still later book of Daniel:
"And at that time shall Michael stand up, the great
prince which standeth for the children of thy people;
and there shall be a time of trouble, such as never
was since there was a nation even to that same time;
and at that time thy people shall be delivered,
every one that shall be found written in the book,
and many of them that sleep in the dust of the earth
shall awake, some to everlasting life and some to
shame and everlasting contempt. And they that be
wise shall shine as the brightness of the firmament;
and they that turn many to righteousness as the
stars for ever and ever."

Throughout the prophets it was the nation that
should be restored, rise again from its ashes, a
thought which does not involve the recall to life of
those myriad Israelites who had long slept with their
fathers. The distinctive promise of the Old Testament is that Israel shall endure for ever, rather than
that its dead shall rise, or individual lives continue
immortally.

But Israel's faith in her restoration by the hand of Yahweh had to adapt itself to the postponement of its realisation, because of the fact of Israel so glaringly unrestored. As that consummation appeared more and more remote, its features ceased to resemble the realities of the past or present. Prophecy became a revelation of the distant and the different, of that which is supermundane if not spiritual : it changed to what is called apocalyptic. No longer drawing its substance from experience, it lost the faculty of presenting reality.

The vision of Ezekiel enters upon these marvels of revelation ; and while the first part of Daniel seems pious fiction, the latter part is sheer apocalyptic. Through the last two pre-Christian centuries and the first century of our era, apocalyptic writings form the most curious, if not most interesting, part of Jewish literature. The writers screen themselves under the holy names of the past : Enoch, The Twelve Patriarchs, Psalms of Solomon, Baruch, Ezra, — even Sibylline Oracles appear. Their compositions do not lack in power and impressiveness ; but such revelations of a grandiloquently restored Israel, when regarded as an adjustment of the human spirit with any probabilities of human lot, are without that reality which is drawn from the arguments of experience.

One element of reality, however, or at least of universal human hope, pressed gradually to expres-

sion in this literature of fantastic and fanatical
adjustment. It was the conviction that at least
the righteous dead should rise again, a conviction
frequently supplemented by the further hope that
the wicked should be punished. As the decades
passed, the conception of the resurrection life of
the righteous tended rather waveringly to rise from
earth to heaven, and to abandon the thought of an
Israel glorified and restored upon a paradisic earth,
for that of a more spiritual kingdom and an eternal
life in heaven. Until that resurrection, which shall
coincide with a final day of God, a true Last Judgement, the spirits of the righteous are at rest guarded
by Angels.[1] In portions of this literature the figure
of a Messiah advances to prominence, becomes the
protagonist of the consummation, the Judge of the
World, a more than human being, — called sometimes the Christ, The Righteous One, "The Son
of Man." [2] Again that figure passes out of view.

Were these conceptions of the resurrection of
Israelitish origin or derived from contact with the
Persian religion ? They were required by the
previous development of Jewish thought, and thus
seem to represent organic growth. In this respect

[1] This is the teaching of the Ethiopic book of Enoch, xci-civ.
See Charles, "Eschatology, Hebrew, Jewish and Christian,"
Second edition.

[2] In the "Similitudes," chapters xxvii-lxx of the Ethiopic
Enoch (94–64 B.C.) Charles, o.c.

they appear as Israel's own, although suggestions may have come from without. On the other hand, the idea of souls entering immediately after death into an immortality of blessedness or perhaps of punishment, as held by Alexandrian Jews, represented draughts of Hellenism. With these Alexandrians, for instance in the Book of Wisdom or the writings of Philo, there is no resurrection of the body, but the soul rises to immortality upon the body's death.

It is not hard to find a sort of spiritual parting of the ways throughout the prophets from Isaiah down to the latest composers of apocalyptic. A parting of the ways as to the purpose and result of the redemption and restoration of Israel: was that to herald the victory and domination of the Jewish nation over the peoples of the earth? or was it intended as a sign to the peoples and the means of spiritual regeneration for the world? These twin conceptions wrestled with each other through Israel's centuries. The one met with overthrow from the legions of Titus and of Hadrian: the other led to Christ.

CHAPTER VI

THE HEROIC ADJUSTMENT IN GREEK POETRY

IT is through no accident that what survives of the literature of Israel is religious and turned toward God, while the great surviving literature of Greece has to do with the wisdom and goodliness of man; for the spiritual stress of either people accorded with the literature that has happily come down to us. Different principles of life, and different ways of arriving at them, made the Greek race illustrious and sanctified the Jew. In Judea, the ways and commands of Yahweh were the sanction of conduct and the crown of life. In Greece, man's adjustment of his life with its anxieties and controlling destinies was by no means unrelated to conceptions of the gods and the sovereign will of Zeus; but it was more constantly moulded through a rational consideration of whatever lay open to perception, and could make part of human knowledge, and be tested by human reason.

The Greek drew confidence and certitude from his temperament and the eagerness of his desires, from consideration of events, and from reflection upon their source and moving causes; also from the serenity arising through the exercise of his body and the intending of his mind. The deed accomplished, or the broad explanatory thought reflected on, could free the Greek from hampering fears, and constitute for him that liberty of life and action which is felicity and peace.

One will find the Greek adjustment as many-sided as the Greek nature, and as manifold as Greek desires. Its varied phases may be followed from Homer, through the lyrical and dramatic poets, to the philosophers. The epic freedom sounding in the heroic temper is succeeded by the more analytically conceived, but still heroic, serenity of the perfect deed of which Pindar sings. One passes readily to the fateful consideration of conduct with Æschylus, Sophocles, and Euripides. But the adjustment of the philosophers seemingly rests on another principle — the satisfaction which for minds capable of large detachment lies in sheer consideration of the universe and man. Yet an Hellenic kinship extends through these adjustments, and a progress will be perceived from those which are simple and almost physical, to those which rest on thought.

Our strict concern is with that adjustment with life and the powers of life which constitutes spiritual freedom. But Greece lures us to wander and admire. Her manifold excellences are so pleasant, so provocative of comment. How can one speak of Homer without dwelling on the grandeur of the Epics, the beauty and elevation of their diction, the living power and measured swiftness of their narratives, their glowing scenes of life and character, all making up that glorious tale of Troy ?

Yet the very excellence of the Epics, the full round of humanity which they set forth, their way of making all things great and beautiful, the eagerness and power of the Heroes, the love of beauty inherent in the poems and in the minds of the *dramatis personæ*, are all pertinent to the Homeric, which is to say, the Heroic, adjustment. Through courage and power of resolve, rather than in their conscious reasoning, Achilles and Odysseus, or Hector and Diomede, present the heroic adjustment with life's fated limitations. And so it is with "Homer" himself, that is to say, with the Epics and their way of inculcating wisdom, not so much by maxim, as by setting forth the tragic courses of events, with some unavoidable pointings of the tale. The narrative itself is pregnant with reflection upon life.

The Homeric adjustment is swung between the realisation (in every sense of the word) of the greatness of man and the shortness and pain of human life. The negative pole is conspicuous enough : "even as the generations of leaves are the generations of men"; men are heavy-fated, δυστήνοι; the gods speak of them as "wretched mortals." The most splendid lives may be the most grievously stricken. "For the gods have made it the lot of wretched mortals to live in affliction while they are without sorrow. Two jars stand on the floor of Zeus filled with evil gifts, and another with blessings. He to whom Zeus gives a mingled lot, at one time encounters evil, at another good. But him to whom Zeus gives of the evil kind he makes a wretch of; hunger drives him over the broad earth, and he wanders honoured neither by gods nor men." So speaks Achilles to Priam; and both knew. The gods interfere to direct the counsels of men, and aid or thwart their endeavours. The masterful will of Zeus intertwines with fate, which is the dumb necessity of things in their common courses, or the appointed, if sad, event of some heroic life.

The positive pole of the adjustment is fixed in the ἀρετή and πινυτή, the *virtus* and *prudentia*, the temper and consideration of the heroes. With each man it is set in the intensity of his passions and desires, in his imaginative or beautifying enhancement of the objects of his wishes, in his strength of will to obtain them, in fine, in his greatness of character. Yet the broad and balanced view belonging to conscious reasoning is rarely absent. For example, the recurring note in the character of Sarpedon, the Lycian king and son of Zeus, is αἰδώς, which is the inbred sense of honour with its complement of shame at all things shameful. Whenever Sarpedon appears, αἰδώς is the motive of his conduct, even as when he calls to the Lycians broken before Patroclus, "Shame on you Lycians; where are you running? Courage! I will withstand the man." Before this day when he went forward to his fate, he had urged on the pensive Glaucus with words which give the argument of this instinct of his nature: "Why, Glaucus, is high honour paid to thee and me in Lycia, and all look on us as gods? and why do we hold a rich and fair domain by the banks of Xanthus? For this we must meet the hot fight with the foremost, that the cuirassed Lycians may say, not inglorious are our kings who rule in Lycia and eat fat sheep and drink sweet wine. Child! if by shunning this battle we should be freed from age and death, I would not fight nor send you into the combat. But since death's myriad shears beset us always, and no man can escape, let us on, and win fame or give it."

Throughout the Epics it is manifest that the sum of a man's impulses, which is his character, is the basis of his opinions and the source of his determination and conduct. Statement and argument are the justification of what his nature has determined. His more intellectual faculties give articulate form to his instinctive adjustment with the powers that constrain his lot. Yet character still intensifies the thought and ennobles the expression of it.

Take the great instances: Hector, Achilles,

Odysseus, Helen! Bunyan might have named the first of these "Greatheart." Courage, devotion, magnanimity, determine Hector's acts and form his adjustment with his fate, ignorant as he is when the gods will slay him at the hands of the Greeks. Through these qualities he is Troy's defence; they likewise transform his disapproving words to Paris into an exhortation to do the duty of a prince. He talks to Helen with the kindliest courtesy; and one cannot speak of the scene with Andromache without drawing it down to the level of our poorer words. A high sense of shame impels him to action, well knowing that the day will come when mighty Troy shall perish; and his dearest grief is the fate that then will fall on his wife and child. Yet he comforts Andromache with the pale thought that no one shall send him to Hades before his time, nor has coward or brave ever escaped his fate. So he answers the cautious Polydamus that he cares not whether the vultures rise on the right hand or the left; he trusts the will of Zeus and the best omen, which is to fight for one's country. Evidently Hector's adjustment with what fate had in store for him is fixed in his courage and temper.

The same is true of a greater hero, whose life is held in fate more definitely than Hector's. The grandeur of the Homeric Achilles should be measured by the greatness of the qualities that are his, and by the moving beauty of their unison in this being so passionate, yet strong in self-restraint, cruel in wrath, tender in love of friend, convulsive in grief, in revenge a raging bane, in sorrow passing the comprehension of other men, then graciously pitying, and withal endowed with the faculty of true consideration. His decisions spring from the heroic temper, from the passion for brave conduct and the glory of it. He could not but make the hero's choice of warfare around mighty Troy, rather than long life. He was easily first in deeds among the Achæans until outrage was put on him by Agamemnon. Then anger thrusts glory from his mind; and under its dulling influence he thinks it were better to sail home to Phthia, comfort himself with a wife, live those long years once conditionally promised him, and for a time escape the stricken lot of Shades. His mind may have been turning, through those hours while he sat quieting his mood by singing the famous deeds of men. But when he hears the words of the Envoys asking aid, anger against Agamemnon again possesses him, and his indignation takes the form of that high argument with which he answers and refuses. Its impetus carries him on to declare that all the wealth of Ilium is no pay for the life of man — "Kine may be had for the harrying, and tripods and horses, but the breath of man comes back neither by raid nor foray, when it once has passed the barrier of his teeth. My mother, Thetis of the silver feet, said that one of two different fates is bringing me to my death : if, staying here, I fight about the city of the Trojans, my return is cut off, but my fame will be imperishable; but if I sail home to my own country, my good fame perishes, but my life shall be long."

Imagine Achilles actually sailing away from the war! The thought leaves him with the violence of his anger. Glory and an early death had been his choice before; and after Patroclus has fallen, when Thetis tells him his fate will follow upon Hector's, though moved, he answers: "Then let me die, since I did not ward off death from my comrade. He perished far from his home, and lacked me to defend him. But now, since I shall not return to my own country, neither was I a light of refuge to Patroclus or the many others who were overcome by divine Hector, but sit by the ships a burden to the earth, may strife perish from among gods and men! . . . I go to meet Hector the destroyer of that dear head: and I will take my death whenever Zeus wills to bring it to pass, and the other gods. For not even the might of Heracles escaped death, though dearest of all to Zeus; but fate overcame him and Hera's hate."

Achilles knows his greatness and his mortality. It is as in words of remorseless fate that he refuses to spare Priam's son, Lycaon: "Fool, speak not to me of ransom! until Patroclus met his fatal day, it was my pleasure to spare the Trojans, and many I took

alive and sold.   But now there is not one that shall
escape death, whom the God gives into my hand
before Ilium.   But, friend, even thou must die.
Why dost thou wail ?   Patroclus is dead, a far
better man than thou.   Dost thou not see how big
I am and goodly ? — sprung from a noble father
and a goddess bore me ?   But upon me as well as
thee lie death and heavy fate.   It may be in the
morning or the afternoon or mid-day, when some one
shall take my life with cast of spear or arrow."

Besides the heroic temper and the mental sight
which is clear as to the event of every life, there is
in Achilles a further nobility of motive, rising, if one
will, from a sense of life's finer fitnesses and the
reverence due to its pitiableness.   As the passions
of grief and vengeance spend themselves, a calm
comes to him through obedience to the gods and
pity for the sorrows of Priam.   When the old man
has clasped the hands which have slain his son, and
Achilles, weeping for his own father and his dead
friend, has raised him up and spoken those words
of high consideration of the lot of man, has placed
Hector's body on the wagon, then with the story of
Niobe he induces in himself and Priam the tragic
calm arising from contemplation of the calamities of
men in their larger aspects.

The heroic temper is also a constant element in
the adjustment presented by Odysseus, but with
an equally constant weighing of life's values.   His

K

adjustment is that of the heroic intelligence. It is achieved by the steadfastness and right action of a much-experienced man, who acts with veritable if canny heroism, with loyalty to his comrades and a full sense of what it behooves him their leader to dare and do for them — the sense of αἰδώς. His hero-spirit flashes ever and anon; never inopportunely. For his nerve is iron. As in the hollow horse he had kept the chiefs from crying out on hearing Helen's voice, so in rags in his own house he can keep his counsel, bear the wooers' insults, watch the shameless maid-servants, and still hold his hand: "Endure, heart! A shamefuller thing didst thou bear on that day when Cyclops devoured thy brave comrades. Then thou didst endure till thy cunning brought thee out from the cavern where thou thoughtest to die."

Odysseus' words always carry the wisdom of experienced intelligence; his admonitions express the convictions of a mature right-minded man. Thus he warns the least evil of the wooers: "Amphinomus, you seem to me intelligent and the son of a good father; so listen to me and consider. Nothing is feebler than man of all that earth nourishes. He thinks ill will never come on him, so long as the gods give him hardihood and sustain his knees! But when the blessed gods bring woes on him, he bears them also, though unwilling! . . . Therefore let no man be wicked, but let him possess in silence the gifts of the gods, whatever they may give."

No man excelled Odysseus in wisdom or in sacrificing to the gods: the two go together. With reverence for the heavenly powers, he checks the shrill joy of the old nurse at the death of the wooers: "In thy heart, old woman, rejoice, nor cry aloud. It is impious to exult over slain men. These the doom of the gods overcame and their evil deeds; for they respected no man. . . . Wherefore through their wickedness they have met a shameful fate." Thus the wisdom of Odysseus takes measure of the heavenly powers.

Perhaps the highest chord of the whole Hellenic adjustment also murmurs in the Odyssey — the joy of satisfying human curiosity, and knowing things. It is the opening note of the poem: "Tell me, muse, of the man, the ready one, who wandered far after he had destroyed the mighty citadel of Troy, and saw the cities of many men, and learned to know their mind." Wherever the hero is cast, he is eager to find out what manner of men live there. Bound to the mast, he listens to the Siren-song — attuned to answer his own nature: "Oh! come hither, renowned Odysseus, glory of the Achæans; stop the ship and hear our voices. For none has ever driven past in his black ship till he has heard from our lips the sweet song, but, having enjoyed it, he sails on, and knowing more.

For we know all things — whatever in the broad
land of Troy, Argives and Trojans suffered at the
will of the gods; and we know whatever happens
on the teeming earth."

And still another more pervasive conception
gave finish and a proportionment of values to the
Homeric adjustment — the thought of beauty, that
which is καλόν, a thought embracing all things
physical, passing over into the sphere of the mind,
and finally reflecting Homer's judgement as to what
was right and proper, most broadly well for man.
The thought of beauty becomes the reflex of Homer's
broadest wisdom. We may even take it as the
moving principle which built the Epics, gave them
their mighty plan, their splendid movement, their
episodic propriety, and perhaps that verity of incident, discourse, and event, through which they
exemplify life's facts and teaching. Homer's people
apply the thought of beauty to the human form and
visage, to trappings and utensils, arms and armour,
horses and chariots, to the lyre of Apollo and the
voices of the Muses, to human speech and conduct.

Beauty, like greatness, may justify and vindicate.
That which not only was seen in Helen's face, but
inhered in every word and act, raised her above
blame. Her mortal grace forbade reproach. She was
divine among women. So Achilles was justified
by his greatness, uplifted above common judgement, but not above mortal fate. Homer was too

wise to condemn great beings, save upon consideration of all their attributes. His ethics included the
proportionment of everything entering life. Helen
speaks of herself and Paris "on whom Zeus has
set such an evil fate that we shall be a theme of
song to men in times to come." Justification, as
well as adjustment, rises from that beauty or that
greatness which is its own excuse for being and
makes a theme of song — a joy to men, a heightening
of knowledge, an expansion of thought. Herein is
the vindication of Achilles, of Helen, and the fate
of Troy —

ὄψιμον ὀψιτέλεστον, ὅου κλέος οὔ ποτ᾽ ὀλείται.[1]

The content which the common man finds in his
daily work or occupation is his practical adjustment.
The strenuous man proceeds more vigorously, and
the high-minded man more ideally, trying to accomplish what seems the best to do, or attain, or be.
This endeavour constitutes his working satisfaction;
herein lies his spiritual freedom — his freedom to
fulfil his nature, his release from fear, his actual
adjustment with life and the eternal ways. Such an
adjustment represents the kinetic principle, the
Aristotelian ἐνέργεια, man's highest energy wherein
he enters on an efficient unison with his best ideals,
attains his freedom and his peace — may even

[1] *Il.*, II, 325. Late and late accomplished, the fame of which
shall never fade.

reach the working peace of God which passes under-standing.

From such a point of view, one may regard the Greek poetic and artistic adjustment, of which the Homeric was the elemental stage. In Hesiod, in the greater lyrists, in the dramatists, at least until Euripides, the elemental poetic adjustment of Homer advances to deeper consciousness, with little change of principle or motive. Like all serious adjustments, whether sounding in active human energy or in contemplation, the adjustment presented in the higher modes of Greek poetry proceeded from an estimate of the facts of human life, their relative permanence, their proportionate values, the possibilities of their attainment, the happiness therefrom arising, and the fitting principles of conduct and regard.

The Greek poetic adjustment accepted the bounds of mortality, while perceiving the greatness of man although held within them. It sprang from the heroic temper, worked itself out through heroic valour and intelligence, and rested in heroic achieve-ment. Primarily heroic, it remained royal or aris-tocratic, suited to those whose nature and position set them above the common mass. Yet as it recog-nised mortality's limitations, its deepest ethics lay in its insistence on the retribution overtaking those who insolently would reach beyond, or impiously transgress the principles of righteousness, which were

thought to rest upon the sanction of the gods, of
Zeus above all.

All this is in Homer; but is developed with
varied temperamental color and profound consideration by Pindar and Æschylus and Sophocles. Before them had come Hesiod, reputed the most
terre-à-terre of the Greek poets — an honest and
religious soul. Impressed with the value of just
dealings among men, he believed that Zeus and the
other gods observed just and evil deeds, rewarding
the one and punishing the other. The just prosper,
their city flourishes, peace is in their borders, their
land bears its crops, their sheep are heavy with
wool, their wives bear children like their parents;
while ill-fortune comes to the wicked (*Works*, 255
sqq.). Not for long could the Greeks hold to this
old crass conviction (for a while held by the Jews !),
which further reflexion must show to be faulty.

Nearer to Pindar were the earlier lyrists, those
who uttered their keen notes of restless but not
unmeasured daring, like Archilochus and Alcæus;
those who were saddened or embittered over life's
mortality, like Mimnermus, or Theognis, in some
of the verses bearing the latter's name : — as for
Sappho, the flames of passion and the love of beauty
made the summit of her being. Apparently the
best adjustment in these poets clung to the principle
of Measure — the widely applicable thought of μηδέν
ἄγαν, which reverted to Hesiod's injunction to ob-

serve measure, and his famous saw, "the half is better than the whole."

Pindar's thought of life, its possibilities and satisfactions, its adjustment with its fated bounds, is more complete. He is in the line from Homer, prizing all the qualities — for the most part coming from φυά, one's inborn nature — which fill out man's greatness, and not those alone which are more especially ethical. He holds to strength and beauty, swiftness, valour, bravery, and apt intelligence; also the wealth and position proper to greatness: an aristocrat altogether. But let not wealth and power overween! It behooves man to seek things suitable (ἐοικότα), such as are meet for mortals, knowing where his feet must come![1] And whatever be his valour or his wit, let him not boast, but remember that success comes from the gods: it is Zeus that gives or withholds.[2] Yet success — from the gods — comes only to those who have striven. Toil and effort — by these means victory is won, and happiness, though man be a thing of a day! From victory comes forgetfulness of toil and anxiousness and death. There are values which do not sound in permanence — like the perfect instant, the perfect deed! That has absolute worth transcending its own briefness; and, crowned by victory, it brings the high mood which is the zenith for mortals, and makes the doer's adjustment with

[1] *Pyth.*, III, 59 *sqq.*   [2] *Pyth.*, III, 103; *Isth.*, IV, 50.

life's limitations and the Powers which set them.[1]
Beyond this, there is also the report which lives after
a man, and reveals his life to the poets, which is
fame.

Pindar is unrivalled in his phrased sententiousness.
And yet more splendidly his fourth Pythian ode
exemplifies these principles in action, telling the
glorious story of Jason and the Golden Fleece,
through which breathes the living truth of the
Pindaric adjustment, drawing its being from the
perfect deed.

Æschylus was a Titan dominated by moral and
religious principles: crimes entail punishment;
right conduct cannot wreck the doer; the Mean is
safest; great prosperity does not of itself bring overthrow, but is apt to beget insolence, with the en-
suing round of crime and ruin. These convictions
were rooted in faith in the punitive and benign rule
of Zeus and the subsidiary divine potencies. The
gods will cast down the proud man who has sinned,
and his overweening children; but suffering shall
bring wisdom to those who act aright, although they
are involved in the fatal dilemmas of a blood-
stained house. This is Zeus's law — a stern fore-
runner of Plato's thought and Paul's announcement,
that to them who love God all things work together for good. The Æschylean adjustment lies
in adherence to these ethical and divine principles,

[1] Cf. *Ol.*, I, 97; II, 56; VIII, 72.

this sequence of the Zeus-supported power of the act working itself out even in pain and blood. Man's proper freedom of action lies within the constraint of these laws; which are incarnate in the story of the house of Atreus.

The *Agamemnon* opens with the weariness of the watchman on the roof at Argos, and the boding anxiousness of the chorus, which is checked rather than lifted by the announcement that Troy has fallen. Too much evil conduct has gone before to allow a happy issue to those enmeshed in this crime-spotted web. Sorrow! Sorrow! may the good prevail!—The chorus can throw off their burden only through appeal to Zeus, who leads mortals to be wise, who has set through suffering the path of wisdom—a kindness enforced. To have summoned Greece to general slaughter for one guilty woman!—a fit prelude to the fatal dilemma of the fleet, wind-bound at Aulis, and no release except through sacrifice of the guiltless for the guilty, of Iphigeneia to win back Helen! That was a sin, by whatsoever stress of need entailed.

The first report is made certain: The Greeks have taken Troy—surely the stroke of Zeus on Paris and on Priam's city. There is no stronghold for him who tramples on sanctities, and in the arrogance of wealth spurns the altar of justice. But what if the guilty have been guiltily destroyed by the avengers? In the place of living men, how many urns of ashes have come back from Ilium! — men fallen because of another's wife! Heavy with anger is the city's voice, filling the function of a public curse. How dangerous is too much glory! Let me neither a captive nor a spoiler be!

It is unnecessary to sketch the action of this (as many think) greatest of all tragedies. It is enough to observe the sequence of recurring crime and more unrighteous vengeance. Clearer becomes the old men's view of that flower of loveliness, that fawning lion's cub of doom, Helen, bane to city, man, and ship. It is not prosperity that brings retribution; the righteous house may remain fair and blessed; it is the sinful act that begets children like itself; the old ὕβρις, when the time is ripe, engenders a new ὕβρις in the wicked which is their doom.

The sequence is quite clear. Cassandra's cry, her utterance becoming more articulate, till she lays bare the tale of ancestral crime, handed on from one generation to another, through conduct never free from guilt — this backward-reaching forward-reaching vision, which raises the *Agamemnon* to the summit of all tragedy, makes plain the scheme of the Æschylean adjustment. She scents the track of crimes done long before, sees the harsh chorus of Erinyes, drunk with human blood, not to be cast out, still chanting that primal impious act, the brother's couch defiled, and then those children slaughtered by their kin, holding out hands filled with flesh, a dish for their own father.

It is thus that the cursed act, an infection for the unborn wicked, passes on through blood; and now with Agamemnon's murder, in which likewise is the will of Zeus, it seizes the blood-guilty Clytemnestra, vaunting her crime, entangling herself in that same curse which she points to as her exculpation.

The Furies are not yet appeased; they shall become those of a mother slain; and then, after purification of the slayer, shall change from curses to potential blessings, from Erinyes to Eumenides. Through the drama of vengeance and that of exculpation, the *Choëphoroi* and the *Eumenides*, the old Greek point of view is to be seen: the mandates and threats of the murdered Agamemnon (through, rather than by virtue of, the oracle of Apollo) drive Orestes to kill Clytemnestra; the son who fails to avenge his father shall be eaten by disease, disowned by all, and cast out from the city to perish vilely.[1] When Orestes is about to kill the murderess, she threatens him with the "hounds of a mother's hate"; at which he demands how can he escape

[1] *Choëph.*, 261 (269) *sqq.* A considerable part of the *Choëphoroi* consists of Electra's and Orestes' invocation of the dead Agamemnon and the mighty curses of the slain to aid them in their vengeance.

his father's, if he forbear to kill her? (*Choëph.*, 910 (925)). When the deed is done, Orestes states in justification that he killed his mother, his father's murderess and an abomination to the gods; and adduces the oracle of Apollo that he should be without blame if he did it, but subject to penalties unnameable if he forbore. With a suppliant's branch, he will go, as Apollo bade him, to the god's shrine for refuge. And he rushes out, pursued by his mother's Furies.

At the opening of the *Eumenides*, Clytemnestra's Furies are asleep around Orestes seated at the central altar of the temple. He has undergone the prescribed rites of purification. Apollo enters with the words, "I will not fail thee," and sends him to Athens under Hermes' guard, there finally to be freed. Orestes leaves the temple as Clytemnestra's ghost rouses the sleeping Furies in pursuit.

Orestes comes to Athene for a final decree of justification, in order that his mother's Furies may cease from troubling him while living, or when he has passed to Hades, a great corrector of impiety below the earth. In a tremendous ode, the Furies chant the Æschylean ethical sequence, fearful as they are lest the old laws be made null, and all restraint removed from crime, if Orestes be acquitted: "There are times when fear is well, abiding as a warder of the mind. Wisdom through suffering profits. What man, what city, freed from dread, will revere justice? Praise thou neither the despot-ridden nor the lawless state. Everywhere God gives might to the Mean. From impiety is born insolence; but from health of mind that fortune much prayed for, dear to all. I counsel thee, always revere the altar of right, nor spurn it with godless foot, thine eyes set on gain. For punishment shall follow, and the fitting end awaits. . . . He who, unforced, is just, shall not be unblest, and never can be utterly destroyed. But the rash transgressor shall in time haul down his yard-arms broken; he calls on those who do not hear in the storm, while the god laughs at the man of boasts, who, failing to weather the point, is wrecked on the reef of Justice, and perishes." [1]

The judgement of Athene, on grounds quite curious to us, takes the case of Orestes out of this sweep of retribution, this sequence whose validity is in no way impugned by the turn of the drama; while the Furies (Erinyes) are placated and won to dwell beneath the Areopagus, as the Eumenides, awarders of blessings for the righteous people of Athene.

Character, good or bad, a criminal or benevolent disposition, either philosophically viewed or tragically treated, is part of the broad matter of human freedom and responsibility, and their compatibility with fate or the divine will or foreknowledge. In-

---

[1] *Eum.*, 490–565, condensed.

herited tendencies, the sins of the fathers visited
upon the children, even the specific curse entailed,
may be regarded as possible elements of our universal mortality, passing down from generation to
generation. A Greek tragedy might present such
elements of life through the spectacle of the unhappy turns of human lot occasioned by them; but
its mode of treatment did not solve, so much as
deepen and render terrible, the mystery of their
action, ethical, divine, physical, or quasi-physical.

Having sought in the great trilogy of Æschylus
for what seemed his mind's adjustment with the
powers of retribution and reward, we turn to look
for the peace of Sophocles in those of his dramas
which have to do with the unspeakable deeds of
Œdipus and the fate of his house. The adjustment
presented by their chief characters is noble and
beautiful. It also is heroic, resting in that high
conduct and temper which belong only to great men
and women. It is thus in line with the Homeric
and Æschylean adjustment, being established in the
might of a rational and temperamental adherence
to powers and principles held to be the most potent
and the best. Its peace is made firm through constancy of noble mood, rather than through the
reasoning processes which support it.

This path of surest satisfaction, which in freedom
of soul a man may tread, is presented in the first
strophe of the ode chanted by the chorus when the

drama of *Œdipus the King* has reached its final
stress of tension, and the discovery is imminent:
"May destiny still find me winning the praise of
reverent purity in all words and deeds sanctioned
by those laws of range sublime, called into life
throughout the high clear heaven, whose father is
Olympus alone; their parent was no race of mortal
men, no, nor shall oblivion ever lay them to sleep;
the god is mighty in them, and he grows not old." [1]

So long as man fulfils this prayer, he is possessed
of the best that comes to man; with peace in his
soul, he is in accord with the mightiest arbiters of
his destiny. But Œdipus unwittingly, and yet
because he was himself, has shattered these laws
through deeds which the tongue refuses to utter.
It may be that no man is evil through unwitting
sin; and that toward such, men's anger softens
(Soph. Frag., 599; *Trach.*, 727). Yet all the absolv-
ing powers of life cannot make Œdipus as if he had
not done these deeds; and as the deeds cannot be
undone, neither can the consequences involved in
them — any more than when a blind man steps off
a precipice, one born blind, say, for a parent's sin!
As easy can a man cease to be himself as throw off
the entailments of his acts. He can only live them
out, as he lives out his life. So the *Œdipus at
Colonus* comes as the drama of the close of a long
expiation, no paltry exculpation by foolish or angry

---

[1] *Œd. Tyr.*, 863–871. Jebb's Translation.

argument; though as against a shameless accuser,
Œdipus can free himself from blame quite over-
whelmingly : "Bloodshed — incest— misery — all
this thy lips have launched against me, — all this
that I have borne, woe is me ! by no choice of mine :
for such was the pleasure of the gods, wroth, haply,
with the race from of old. Take me alone, and
thou couldst find no sin to upbraid me withal, in
quittance whereof I was driven to sin thus against
myself and against my kin. Tell me, now, — if,
by voice of oracle, some divine doom was coming
on my sire, that he should die by a son's hand, how
couldst thou justly reproach me therewith, who was
then unborn, whom no sire had yet begotten, no
mother's womb conceived ? And if, when born to
woe, as I was born, I met my sire in strife, and slew
him, all ignorant what I was doing, and to whom,
— how couldst thou justly blame the unknowing
deed ?" [1]

Thus the blind old man strikes away the ground
from his accuser's feet; but not thus would he cut
the ground away from fact. He had said with
deeper truth : "My deeds have been sufferings
rather than acts." Long fellowship with sorrows,
and a noble nature have brought resignation.
Through bearing thus the consequences of his deeds,
he attains his peace. At last he is accepted by the
Powers which absolve and consecrate. At the

[1] *Œd. Col.*, 962–977. Jebb's Translation.

L

thunder signal, understood by him, he rises, and with no need of guidance for his sightlessness, moves onward to the place where he may hide his life with the dead, or rather where, somehow from the gods, the lower world opens for him in kindness, without pain: his passing "was not with lamentation or in sickness and suffering, but above mortal's wonderful."

After the death of Œdipus, the accursed fratricidal struggles of his sons were doomed to come, and draw to a devoted death that perfect flower of Greek womanhood, Antigone. Like the tale of Œdipus or Agamemnon, her story needs no telling. Antigone's adjustment was Antigone; it lay in her character, her essential being; an adjustment of an heroic woman's perfect devotion, her perfect following of the best. Its power was her high constant mood, supported by the reasonings of her mind, but scarcely needing them. Though death must follow, there is neither hesitation nor need of any prior dialectic stimulation in her resolve to bury her brother's corpse. She, being herself, could not fail so to resolve and act, — καλόν μοι τοῦτο ποιούσῃ θανεῖν, she tells her weaker sister, Ismene: "Well for me to die doing this; as a loved one I shall lie with him, a loved one, sinless in my crime; since what I must do to satisfy the dead is for a longer time than what is owed the living: *there* I shall lie forever." And when the helpless act is done, and

Antigone is to die, she bids Ismene, now vainly seeking to have part with her: "Be of good cheer; thou livest; but my soul died long ago, so that I might serve the dead."

The drama turns upon the conflict between the ruler's decree, the law proclaimed by man, and those higher laws and sanctities established in the divine order, — which Roman jurists and the Middle Ages were to recognise as the *lex naturalis*. They have been acclaimed in the *Œdipus Tyrannus;* and now as against Kreon's decree, which Antigone admits having wilfully disobeyed, she appeals to them: "For it was not Zeus that had published me that edict; not such are the laws set among men by the justice who dwells with the gods below; nor deemed I that thy decrees were of such force, that a mortal could override the unwritten and unfailing statutes of heaven. For their life is not of to-day or yesterday, but from all time, and no man knows when they were first put forth.

"Not through dread of any human pride could I answer to the gods for breaking *these*. Die I must, — I knew that well even without thy edicts. But if I am to die before my time, I count that a gain: for when any one lives, as I do, compassed about with evils, can such a one find aught but gain in death?

"So for me to meet this doom is but a trifling grief; but if I had suffered my mother's son to lie in death an unburied corpse, that would have grieved me." [1]

To disobey a ruler's decree, in order to follow the law of conscience, seemed to the chorus of old Thebans, even in this clear case, a questionable course. A halting sympathy, tending to disapproval, leaves Antigone hapless, despairing almost, as she is led to her living tomb, "unwept, unfriended, without marriage-song." Unhappy, she is still convinced, — if these judgements of men are pleasing to the gods, why, she may learn her fault hereafter! Her last utterance is of noblest poise and truth: "Behold, princes of Thebes, the last daughter of your kings, what I suffer, and from whom, because I revere piety." That was her adjustment.

As an expression of the human adjustment with the powers controlling human destiny, sculpture and painting cannot be as definite as poetry, which has language for its medium. Nevertheless, for those who have the interpretive imagination, an impressive temperamental adjustment lies in the remains of the noblest Greek sculpture: that of the greatness of man in spite of fate, and with an added element of serenity, which it is sculpture's prerogative to express in a pre-eminent degree.

The remains of the sculptures of the Parthenon exemplify this adjustment. Their general theme

---

[1] *Ant.*, 450–468, Jebb's Translation.

was the greatness of Athens, attained (according to the fond Periclean-Phidian ideal) through reverence for the gods as well as through human intelligence, valour, and self-sacrifice; and a greatness likewise to be rejoiced in fittingly and righteously. On the east pediment, Athene breaks into full and potent being; on the west, she conquers Poseidon in vindication of her pre-excellent claim to be recognised as the goddess of Athens. The metopes show Olympian gods victorious over earth-born giants, Greeks conquering Amazons, Lapiths defending the sanctity of their marriage-festival against brutal Centaurs, and, it may be, Athenians victorious over Persians: victories of mind and civilisation and freedom over their brutal or slavish opposites.

So there was rendered the divine and human struggle through which safety and order and freedom were attained, and also, in Athene's birth, the glorious inception of her city's destiny. Finally, the frieze pictured the serene beauty of Athens' present, her youths and stately maidens, her wise elders, and the presence of the gods abiding there. Athens has achieved; in human power and in reverence for the gods she is most bravely blessed. Rhythms of sculptured harmony reflect the discipline and self-control, the temperance and grace of spirit, which, ideally viewed, formed the serene greatness of her civic state — her corporate adjustment with her destinies.

CHAPTER VII

GREEK PHILOSOPHERS

BEING Greeks, the early Greek philosophers cared for much that entered the heroic ideals of the epic and dramatic poets. We are not to take too narrowly their main aspiration, which was to know and understand. For they were not recluses, but members, often active, leading, or even revolutionary, of city-states; and while they sought knowledge for the satisfaction which lay in knowing, the search was well related to the business of human living. Their human ideal looked to the fulfilment of the whole rational man, and included all objects which the intellect might commend. Yet of this whole, the wisdom which is assimilated knowledge was the noblest portion, that which in itself could satisfy, and without which the other human felicities either were unattainable, or, if quickly grasped, were likely to prove worthless. Knowledge was the test and standard, as well as the necessary guide, of life.

Accordingly the deliverance of the human spirit which lies in early Greek philosophy — its liberation from anxieties unto its freest being — pertains to investigation, contemplation, and reflexion, rather than to heroic action, or to material or emotional gratification: it is the θεωρητικὸς βίος, the *vita contemplativa*. With the very earliest of these philosophers, this *vita* lay in the function of curiosity engaged in observing, θεωρία in the primary sense of looking at things, but with the mind's eye as well as with the bodily organ. If one enquires what they were looking at or looking for, it may be answered, they were looking for the stable cause, source rather, of the changing things about them, including their mortal selves. That, once discerned, would satisfy their intellectual natures, since it would provide a basis for all life and the thought about it; would thus prove for themselves a sure intellectual satisfaction.

The well-known names of these men may be mentioned, if only to make sure that there were ideas and temperamental elements common to them all, which will justify some generalisation as to *their* views and *their* adjustment. Certainly the opinions of those first open-eyed and open-minded Ionians — Thales, Anaximander, Anaximenes — did not agree; and the thoughts of the Ephesian Heracleitus differed from them deeply. Still more fundamentally the physics of Parmenides and Zeno differed from the scheme of Heracleitus. They were Western Greeks, called Eleatics after Greek Elea founded in an Italy not yet Italian. That the hypotheses of all these men differed is not the point, but rather that they were all impelled to investigate and consider, and seek satisfaction in the contemplation of the world and in the strength of their meditations.

The three first-named were citizens of Miletus, a powerful and rich and active-minded city of Asia Minor. Yet not alone within its walls, but through this Ionia, both insular and of the mainland, in the seventh and following centuries, curiosity was sleepless, and the mind moved toward θεωρίη, φιλοσφίη, and ἱστορίη — physical observation, speculation, and the human story. Thus it was in Ionia, and when colonies of these Ionians sailed westward, where cities might be founded in a benignant land, far from the power of Lydians and Persians, the colonists did not change their minds by changing the skies above them.

The opinions of these early Greek thinkers about the world are not to be despised, just because we deem ourselves some points closer to the great infinite truth of things than they. What should we think about the world if we were to regard it newly, with no advantage from the range of thought behind us, including the opinions of these very men? From the fragmentary remains and corrupt reports of them, it is hard to ascertain even their main tenets, and impossible to do more than hazardously imagine their data and methods of reasoning. Each facet of their thinking, as when they thought of Sun and Earth, had not the significance of the like-named symbols, when we use them in our thoughts. The same words have other meanings now.

Yet one cannot read the reports concerning them, and the fragments of their utterances, without realising the largeness of their thinking; and if their ideas seem crude and curious, we also know how they passed into the theories of Plato and Aristotle, to be made over or furbished up so as to be presentable to the human mind for ever since. And a still more vital bond between us and them lies in the assumption, which may well be an assurance, that as common intellectual appetitions tended to unite their minds, so the circle of human unity may readily extend to include those even among ourselves who find contentment in research and meditation. These men are gone, and but seeming dust remains of the philosophies with which their thoughts were occupied and their lives made free. Yet it is pleasant for us, who know too many things and not enough, to turn back to elemental hypotheses and feel the ancestry of the men who devised them.

The first matter of the world is water, said Thales; and tradition assures us of the constancy with which his mind was busied with the phenomena of the earth and heavens, while he also abstracted his thoughts through geometry. Likewise, apparently, his hearer Anaximandros, and then Anaximenes, found satisfaction in an elemental main hypothesis, while it is also plain that each of them kept his mind active upon nature's curious phenomena. What kind of investigation and imagination brought the former to assert that living creatures came from the moist element as it was evaporated by the sun, and that man was like a fish in the beginning ? or led the latter to pregnant conceptions of world-formation through rarefaction and condensation ? Then how did the problematic Pythagoras come by his thought of transmigration, for example ? He, too, took comfort in geometry and numbers, and realised how deeply numerical relationships enter the core of things. His possible contemporary, Xenophanes, seems to have won his soul's content by raising within himself an idea of God, neither in form or thought like mortals, but sheer sight and thought and hearing; toilless and moveless, ruling by his thought. Did he find satisfaction also in the sense that the gods had not revealed all things in the beginning? It was for man to seek and find in time what was the better. Was not that indeed the blessed sweat of his mind, by which he should truly live ?

Perhaps the same was felt by the oracular Heracleitus, who said that "Nature loves to hide," or remain hidden, for the Greek verb is in the middle voice. He lashed the stupidity of others, — of the common many who neither know nor learn, also

even of those, reputed wise, who mistake knowing
many things for understanding; perhaps most particularly all those who would not listen to his own
satisfying doctrine that everything entrains its
opposite, becomes its opposite, and in truth is its
opposite, or at least cannot exist without its opposite. There can be no One without a Many, to
speak in later phrase. Conversely, if there be a
conversely, the strife of opposites is equally an
attunement, a procreation — war is father of all.
So all things pass into each other: the world, un-
created by god or man, is an everlasting rekindling
fire-transformation: in this the God is day as well
as night, summer as well as winter, both death and
life.

Was there not enough adjustment for this man
in such a conception of the universe? Especially
when he saw law and measure permeating the eternal
flux, and in human affairs recognised the abundant
flow of law divine from which human laws are fed,
and in the individual man perceived that his character was his fate?

Such thoughts made this man's peace and freedom; as likewise did the thought of Parmenides
for him. From opposite convictions the two drew
equal satisfaction — the one resting in the conception of ceaseless change, the other in that of per-
manent and solid being. This other was grandly
reliant on his thought about things — as he thought,

so must they be; so must Being be: "for it is the same thing that can be thought and that can be." Thought and thought's end or source are the same. Hence existence, which is a moveless corporeal *plenum*, conforms to the philosopher's necessary thought of it. Comfort enough here! There is neither coming into being, nor passing away. It is interesting to note that Parmenides, with his "Greek" love of the definite, conceived his *plenum* of being as a finite, though eternal, sphere. But his follower, Melissus, saw the impossibility of spatial limit to reality.

One is obliged to mention that strange wonder-worker, and yet scientific investigator and philosopher, Empedocles of Agragas, with his fateful four elements, which were really six. For to the four must be added Love and Strife, Love the mixer, Strife the separator and refashioner — two efficient causes, comments Aristotle, and yet material, being themselves measurable portions of the brew.

The difficulty, as it would seem, of conceiving force or agency save as a ponderable corporeal thing, was a pregnant confusion, out of which Greek thought was destined most profitably to rise. The process of this evolution, as yet incomplete, appears in the nimble and potent agency of formative creation which Anaxagoras devised and designated by the name of Nous, the Greek word for *mind*. It was he who came to Athens on Pericles' invitation, doubtless to his advantage, and yet also to be the first of the philosophers persecuted by that jealous and suspicious *demos*. Holding, as he did, that all things are constituted of an infinite number of infinitesimal seeds, so that all things are in everything, and no thing is so small as not to partake of all, holding to this view, he felt the need of an efficient Arranger of the infinite constituent seeds of things, something apart from them. And thus he describes it:

"All other things partake in a portion of every thing, while Nous is infinite and self-ruled, and is mixed with nothing, but is alone, itself by itself. For if it were not by itself but were mixed with anything else, it would partake in all things if it were mixed with any . . . and the things mixed with it would hinder it, so that it would have power over nothing in the same way that it has now, being alone by itself. For it is the thinnest of all things and the purest, and it has all knowledge about everything and the greatest strength; and Nous has power over all things, both greater and smaller, that have life. And Nous had power over the whole revolution, so that it began to revolve in the beginning. And it began to revolve first from a small beginning; but the revolution now extends over a larger space, and will extend over a larger still. And all the things that are mingled together and separated off and distinguished are all

known by Nous. And Nous set in order all things
that were to be, and all things that were and are
not now and that are, and this revolution in which
now revolve the stars and the sun and the moon,
and the air and the æther that are separated off.
And this revolution caused the separating off, and
the rare is separated off from the dense, the warm
from the cold, the light from the dark, and the dry
from the moist. And there are many portions in
many things. But no thing is altogether separated
off nor distinguished from anything else except
Nous. And all Nous is alike, both the greater
and the smaller; while nothing else is like any
thing else, but each single thing is and was most
manifestly those things of which it has most in
it." [1]

Nous is thus a moving, ordering, and knowing
substance. With but a mechanical mentality it is
not yet sheer immaterial mind. Yet it is groping
thither — dreaming on thoughts to come. We
may be sure of its vital importance in the scheme of
thought wherein this philosopher found his content. And as for the man's effect, one perhaps may
say that he started the Mind on its career as Demi-
urge, and made way for the conception of the
Divine Will as Creator of the Universe.

Early Greek thought, unspiritualised in its con-

[1] Translation taken from J. Burnet's *Early Greek Philosophy*,
p. 301 (2d Ed., 1908), to which the writer is otherwise indebted.

ceptions, and looking to matter as the primeval
source, might well regard matter and being as co-
extensive.   Matter and no-matter, conceived as
equivalent to Being and no-Being, led to the Eleatic
denial of motion, the most universal fact of observation as well as the necessary postulate of any
explanation of the World.   An escape from this
dilemma was furnished by the Atoms of Leucippus
and Democritus, infinite in number, indivisible, of
every shape, possessing the eternal and indestructible
qualities of the Eleatic Being, but separated from
each other by narrow fissures of space, and in ceaseless motion.   Their falling whirl produced the
natural forms of the visible Kosmos, and even the
souls of men, which consisted of fiery atoms having
the liveliest motion.[1]

There is no need to say more of this mightiest
and most fruitful of all Greek physical hypotheses,
the substance of which apparently Leucippus
delivered to Democritus.   But the latter extended
and coördinated and humanised philosophy as none
had done before him.   How can one sum up such a

[1] The notions of matter and reality or existence not having
been distinguished before Leucippus's time, he could predicate the
existence of empty space only in uncouth and equivocal terms.
He had to say that *what is not* (*i.e.* not matter) is of no less
account than *what is* (*i.e.* matter), and "that both are alike the
causes of things that come into being." Simplicius quoting
from Theophrastus — Diels, *Fragmente der Vorsokratiker*, 2d Ed.,
Bd. I, p. 345, and trans. by Burnet, *Early Greek Phil.*, p. 384.

man from the fragments that remain of his many and admirable books, — of whom Aristotle says that no one had so profoundly considered growth and change ? His was a prodigious vision, a vision of the mind, inductive, microscopic, penetrating to the infinitesimal, and extending to an infinitude of worlds beyond the range of mortal eye. It is hard for us to make his fiery soul-atoms think; but we are amazed at his insight into the ways of the apprehending mind, as when he distinguished between the "primary" and "secondary" qualities of objects. Busied with physical investigations, he fruitfully recognised the need to consider the differences between the convincing apperceptions of the atoms of his soul and the confusions issuing from the atoms of sensation. Although he did not, like his very different contemporary Socrates, try his thought in the dialectic of definition, he formed a canon of principles by which to discriminate between the means and method of true knowledge and the ways of fallacious opinion, springing from the five senses.

Rational knowledge became for this man the standard not only of thinking but of living. Before its bar he endeavoured to order the contents of life, — whatever entered into human welfare or misery. While his fundamental physical hypotheses held to the laws of that necessity which left no place for divine interposition, he yet evolved from his clearly graduated discrimination a finely spiritualised ethics. Knowledge, virtue, happiness, were at one in his scheme of life. "From understanding proceed good counsel, unerring speech, and right conduct." With him, thought and intent are always the criterion, and the good things of the spirit are more divine. "Happiness and misery are of the soul." A contented mind makes the best life for man; tempering one's will to avoid the tumult of desire. "Goodness lies not merely in doing no wrong, but in wishing to do none." "A man should be most ashamed before himself." For all men, education in virtue is better than the constraint of laws.

A cheerful soul was this Democritus, who said that a "life without its festivals was a long road without an inn to rest at." But a veritable monarch in his thought was he, who desired knowledge rather than the wealth of the Great King, and knew that "to the wise man the whole earth is open; for the Universe is the fatherland of a noble soul." Thus his temper and philosophy made a large adjustment, a home of peace, a spring of freedom for this great-minded man.

The immediate antecedent of Plato is Socrates; but Plato's philosophy holds all prior and contemporary Greek thought and feeling, from Thales to the Sophists and Plato's own generation of Socrates' supposed disciples, and from Homer to Euripides and Aristophanes. A further fringing background for his

M

thought is the supposed traditional wisdom of the older Mediterranean world.

The Sophists played an educational rôle, and also introduced an analytic self-consciousness into Greek thinking. But their exaggerated insistence upon the individual as the measure of all values, including truth, loosed men from their proper anchorages in moral conviction and philosophic certitude. No veritable adjustment, no surety of spiritual freedom, could come through such intellectual dissipation.

Save by reaction. That gained moral force and took dialectic form in Socrates, and flowered with many a dazzling hue in Plato. We have all known the former from our childhood; none the less is he an enigma. Undoubtedly this keenest of questioners so conducted his inquiries as to lead on and up to well-defined conceptions; and undoubtedly in this way he deepened the self-consciousness and self-criticism of philosophic thinking. So, no one disputes the measured words of Aristotle which ascribe to him the inductive method and general concepts or definitions. We also believe that, with unswerving ethical earnestness, he strove constantly, through this method, and making use of the resulting definitions, to arrive at laws of conduct valid for all men, because founded on conceptions true for all. With confidence, finally, we ascribe to him the principle that wisdom and virtue are the same: true knowledge must produce right conduct; since no one errs or sins willingly. This, at all events, was true of Socrates himself, and made the basis of his adjustment in that fearless and rational freedom of right conduct, which has held the admiration of mankind.

Cicero's memorable statement, that Socrates called Philosophy down from the heavens and established her in the abodes of men, and, as we say, set her upon the study of man, is eulogy which Socrates may well deserve, but which, in justice, he must share at least with Democritus and the Sophists.

A number of gifted human beings seem bound together in the personality of Plato; and the adjustment wherein so manifold a nature could bring its different faculties to harmonious action had need to include more than one field of satisfying activity, more than one fount of peace. Plato was hotly in love with mortal beauty; and doubtless often had to bridle what we of northern climes and modern times might call his sensuality. More constantly, however, the image-building, story-building imagination of this poet and dramatist, superseding the importunities of sense, dispersed his passion in poetic myths, or employed his faculties in dramas of the mind, with plots formed from the stress and pitfalls of dialectic. Plato's desires change and are transfigured as they pass from the lower to the higher planes of his nature. Its topmost needs were those of its metaphysical energies; its sublimest insistency was as to the reality of mind and the validity of concepts mentally visualised, and tested, if not formed, by an argumentation which might be destructive or constructive, severe, stupendous, whimsical, but captivating usually, and always carried forward by a resistlessly creative imagination.

What other man ever had such joy in the work and play of his mind as Plato! Here was his real absorption, his real deliverance — that which veritably made his spiritual freedom and his peace. It satisfied him, and he trusted it. His was a great faith. His confidence was absolute in the convictions of his mind, as well as in the certainty of the realisation of its imperative demands. Magnificent as was his dialectic, strenuous as might be its arguments, Plato's faith was pinned to none of them. While willing to follow whither the living and breathing argument might lead, he may be no more serious in his reliance on its procedure or conclusion, than he is upon the truth of the illustrative tales he knows so well to weave. For, as the precursor of all that after him might be named Platonic or Neoplatonic, he is always conscious that no argument can compass the whole truth — of which the processes of dialectic mirror the broken rays. Throughout the *Dialogues*, his parables, whether parables of the poetic imagination or the less obvious parables of dialectic, change and pass; and while he may have been earnest with them at the time, they remain but tentative, open to refutation, ready to be exchanged for something truer or more illuminative. None the less was he insistent that his convictions should be set in reason, should be reasoned out through argument — if that were only possible!

The most famous and influential form assumed by Plato's conviction of the absolute reality of things spiritual was the "Platonic Idea." The mind contemplates the universals in all things, sees them everywhere. With Plato, these type-ideas, from existing solely in the mind, likewise transcend it, and are beheld as absolute spiritual entities, and as the creating shaping powers of the objects of sense-perception — which are their creatures or images. Noblest and realest of all is the idea of the Good, the most absolute of ideal prototypes as well as perhaps the most universal plastic power. Shall it not be as God, — the Fashioner of the World, the Measure of all things?

With Plato, the conceptions of the mind are likewise the desires of his soul. His spiritual nature flows out to them desirously, yearning to bring them to realisation in his soul. This is the soul's health and well-being, its blessed happiness: to mirror and realise within itself beauty, justice, goodness, the excellence of every virtue. In this realisation, this making real, are set the freedom and the peace of Plato, the blessed mood which sometimes we also may gain from reading the *Phædo* or the *Phædrus*, the *Gorgias* or the *Theatætus*.

One sees how Plato's ethical convictions, whether received from his master, or his very own, have root in these conceptions of the mind which are also the desires of his soul. Knowledge and Virtue are the same: How can one know these beautiful ideas and not desire them? and not realise them? Only through knowing them imperfectly can one sin or err. And again, even more obviously, justice is an excellence of the soul, of man's veritable self: it is almost a truism — if only the world would accept it — that the unjust man cannot be in a state of well-being, cannot be veritably happy. The best that can come to him is to be punished, which is to be healed. How then can one doubt that it is better to suffer, than to do, injustice? Or how can any harm whatever be his who has realised that Best within him which is the idea of the Good? Or, in common words, how can ill come to a good man? And as for truth, — is it not the verity of the good? how shall one not crave it and esteem it always?

Plato's freedom dwelt in these convictions, and in his faith in them. As he grew older, he held with increasing assurance that the world is ruled by Mind, and not left, a chance medley, to unreason (*Philebus*). Did not God create it, and create it because he was good, and form it somehow in the

likeness of God, and with a soul throughout its
being? (*Timæus*). In his earlier as well as later
Dialogues, he assumes the existence of the spiritual
when he is not engaged in proving it: the conviction of the reality and the eternal indestructibility
of the human soul abides with him, and he in it.
It was Plato who added this philosophic conviction
of immortality to the human adjustment lying in the
θεωρητικὸς βίος — the search and contemplation of
truth. In one dialogue at least (*Phædo*) he argues
with clear austerity that only after separation from
the body can the soul attain its fairest being in
knowledge of the truth.

The Platonic ideal, which the Platonic faith
realises and transforms into the Platonic deliverance
of the soul, lies — if one dare make any such
assertion as to this Protean genius — in the complete and beautiful perfecting of the soul, which is
man's spiritual and immortal part: the perfecting
of it in the knowledge of virtue and the virtue of
knowledge; the rendering of the soul perfect and
fair, in truth and in right conduct, in geometry
and music and dialectic (with fitting conceptions of
the Universe and its Maker) as well as in courage
and justice. The things of the world of sense-
perception have their value too, giving temperate
pleasure and satisfaction to the outer man, and to
the soul as well, so long as they head no revolt
against its leadership. All these phases of human

concern are included, and the lower subordinated
to the higher, in that consideration of life and its
regulation, which Plato wrote in his last years, and
called the *Laws*. It holds the soul and God
above all, and impresses one as the most devout and
religious composition of the classic world. If it
suffers somewhat from an octogenarian prolixity, it
has broader human wisdom than the much earlier
Republic. It contains the last turns of Plato's
thinking and will be found a storehouse of Aristo-
telianism (that virtue is a mean is in it), and later
thought.

No more than in the case of Plato, is there any
need for us to attempt a statement of the contents
of Aristotle's system. We have but to consider
the end, or rather spring, of his philosophy — the
final cause, if one will use the term, by reason of
which he philosophised, and through which this
most prodigious of philosophers found his satisfaction.

Aristotle clearly stated his ideal of the noblest and
most satisfying, as well as the most divine, mode of
life that man can reach : and then he exemplified
this ideal in himself, and demonstrated that it held
his best freedom of action, his best activity, his
actualisation, his ἐντελέχεια, the fulfilment of himself in the attainment of his final end and actuality.
This was, of course, the life of mind, and pre-
eminently of the mind fixed upon the contemplation

of ultimate causes; while from this highest function of the soul, the true activities of man sloped downward, broadening to a base of virtues which are rooted, and also have their end, in character and conduct.

Aristotle's intellect penetrated every province of investigation. He drew all human knowledge to himself, added to it from his own thinking and research, and stamped the whole indelibly with the methods through which he mastered it and the forms in which he apprehended it. Which province satisfied him best, is hard to tell, even though he says that a knowledge — the investigation — of final causes is the most delightful. Nor, perhaps, is it right to decide this point by the result of his labours, estimated in the light of our present views upon the universe and human society. Speaking from this standpoint, we might term him (in our presumption) an unhappy physicist, especially in astronomy fatally reactionary, and blind to those conceptions of his time which proved themselves the best. In the further realm of metaphysics (more properly named ontology), no one would dare not call him great. Then in the constructive analysis and classification of the forms and categories of valid statement, he was, for good or ill, for mental discipline or sterilisation, the creator of formal logic. Further, he wrote most notably upon the Soul or Life of man, and of its faculties and ways of apprehension. Then, wonderful to say, with powers unimpeded by such preoccupations and sometimes even detached from them, he was a great biologist, pre-eminent as a classifier of living organisms, and as a comparative anatomist and embryologist. Finally, how can we think him less interested in human society and human conduct, and in the arts which captivate and delight men? — seeing that he composed a work on Ethics rightly admired by many generations of mankind, and a work on Politics of enormous influence, and also works on Rhetoric and the Art of Poetry. No, we will not presume to say in what department of intellectual creation this stupendous Aristotle took the keenest joy, but simply recall to mind certain of his statements and bits of his exposition of human nature and its proper functions, wherein he shows at once his ideal of happiness, and the method of his spiritual freedom.

That which man always seeks for its own sake, as a final end, is his happiness, his well-being, — εὐδαιμονία. It is this which suffices of itself, and makes life desirable. It is man's true self-fulfilment, through the proper activity or functioning of his nature. But his nature, or, if one will, his life, is in part shared by the plants and the animals other than man, all obviously below him in the scale of being. That which is his unshared own, and the best that is in him, is his rational intelligence, which most clearly knows itself and is most amply self-conscious. Or we may say this highest part of man is the highest part of that which constitutes his organic life, or, rather, the first stage of its actualisation or fulfilment, its first ἐντελέχεια, to wit, his soul. For soul, with Aristotle, is most comprehensive, and means the life of the whole human organism taking its first form, entering indeed upon a composite self-realisation, to wit, of its nutritive and sensitive faculties, as well as its faculty of thought.

So the highest and most peculiar and proper part of man and of his soul or life, is intelligence. But that, like all of life, is an activity, or at least actualises or fulfils itself as an activity, and not as a passive state. Life is action, and the highest part of life consists in the self-conscious action of the understanding. And herein consists man's εὐδαιμονία, — his final end and happiness, — and from our present point of view, his peace and freedom and deliverance.

Let us make this more explicit. The rational part of the soul or life of man, the ψυχῆ, is twofold, practical and contemplative. The practical ψυχῆ is occupied with contingent changing things, which may be affected by our action; the contemplative is directed to the speculative knowledge of that which is of necessity and changeless. These psychic faculties, termed respectively, if one will, prudence

and wisdom, represent the practical, or ethical, and
the speculative virtues, though the term virtue is
usually appropriated to the former. The practical
virtues are requisite for the happiness of man as a
social animal. They do not come through instruction as much as through constant practice, thereby
becoming ingrained as habits of conduct, which,
inasmuch as they spring from reason or obey it,
are to be deemed purposeful or selective. Their
characteristic is the avoidance of excess, or the pur-
suance of the proper mean, in conformity to the
conduct and opinions of the best men. For their
practice, moreover, opportunity is needed, and some
moderate supporting share of material goods.

To a less, but still to some, degree, material goods
are needed for that highest happiness which consists in the enduring activity of the speculative
reason, and has solely knowledge as its end. It is
sought for the sake of no advantage beyond itself,
and thus is free from all practical and contingent
aims. Well we know that Aristotle was a lover of
all knowledge, even of the meanest creatures and
their smallest functions. And yet this man of
universal intellectual appetition, who recognised
something wonderful in every work of nature,
desired to rise from these broad low fields of knowledge of the caused and changeable to the investigation and contemplation of the changeless causes,
in their uncontingent absoluteness:—surely the

freest of all sciences and the most self-sufficing, and
its votaries the freest of mankind, and the most
divine, the most like God.

For God, in Aristotle's scheme of physics and
ontology, as well as in his consideration of human
and divine happiness, is the moveless mover, drawing all things through their desire for the supreme
Good that he is. But he is also the Contemplator
par excellence; and if the Contemplator, what should
be worthy of his contemplation save Himself?
Therefore the man who leads the life of knowledge
is like God, and he whose mind is fixed, so far as
may be possible for man, upon the causes of all being,
is most like God.

The highest pleasure forms part of this highest
happiness. Happiness is an active energy; and
pleasure ($\dot{\eta}\delta o\nu\dot{\eta}$) is part and parcel of its true and
unimpeded action, its perfecting, its $\tau\epsilon\lambda\epsilon\dot{\iota}\omega\sigma\iota\varsigma$.
Pleasure thus perfects ($\tau\epsilon\lambda\epsilon\dot{\iota}o\iota$) the energy ($\dot{\epsilon}\nu\epsilon\rho\gamma\epsilon\hat{\iota}a\nu$)
which is happiness and which is life. It is so closely
part of the perfect energising of the energy, that one
need not ask which is loved for the other's sake.

The progress of Greek thought did not cease with
Aristotle; but its energies separated into several
channels. Astronomy, mathematics, physics, botany,
through Theophrastus, Aristarchus, Eratosthenes,
Hipparchus, Ptolemy, Euclid, and Archimedes, were
still to make notable advance; and these pursuits
brought peace to the keen minds absorbed in

them. But on the other hand, philosophy, properly or popularly so-called, lost its balanced universality. Plato and Aristotle, while profoundly conscious of the relation of philosophic knowledge to man's practical well-being, loved knowledge absolutely, for its own sake and for the joy of it. But Stoicism, a partial exotic, since its founder Zeno was a Syrian, had narrower interests. It regarded knowledge as a means; ethics, with human well-being as its practical end, was the real Stoical concern. Altered political and social conditions were among the causes of this change. As the city-states gave way to huge Hellenistic kingdoms, which were in turn to yield to Roman rule, men realised their political impotence, and felt but a loosened interest in public affairs. It was enough for them to keep their lives clear of misfortune. And so philosophy, its spirit somewhat quelled with the contracted freedom of its votaries, turned from the search for independent and objective truth, and concentrated its efforts on that which should insure to the philosophic individual a happy life, or one free from pain. In Stoicism, philosophy became a palpable adjustment of human conduct with the Stoic view of human nature and the nature of the world, and a self-conscious endeavour after that freedom which is peace. The same may be said of Stoicism's apparent opposite, Epicureanism, which was also a sheer adjustment, and did not strive as strenuously as its rival to base its practical principles upon a knowledge of man and the world he dwelt in. Both systems thus endangered the progress of that with which they really were concerned. For whenever the enthusiastic and apparently disinterested quest of knowledge weakens, ethics loses the enlarging basis of increasing wisdom needed for ethical advance.

But in the meanwhile, in its Greek periods before it became adapted to the Roman temperament, Stoicism looked earnestly to the constitution of the universe for a basis of its conviction that reason is man's essential nature, and that his sole good consists in acting according to its dictates : such action is virtue, which thus becomes a thing of reason and of the firm will to act in accord. But human reason is part of the reason of the universe, part of universal law, which likewise is felt to be the law or will of God — all-ruling, all-permeating, moving everything with purpose as with power, suiting and harmonising each with all.

Viewing Stoicism from this end, one wonders to find its ethics set in a materialistic conception of the universe, including God and the human soul and virtue itself : all being is material ; the universe, including God and man, consists of matter in a state of tension, or, if one will, of passive matter complemented by its activity of force. God is this force or law, all-moving, all-commingling, moulding all things to their proper ends. The human soul is part of this force, this law, this soul of the universe, which is God. It is diffused like warm breath throughout the body, and though it may for a while continue individual after the body's dissolution, it will eventually be resolved into the world-soul. Its master part, its truest activity, is reason.

Thus, having doubtless leapt over many inconsistencies, we are back at reason and human conduct rationally directed by the will, which is virtue and man's sole good and happiness. All else is indifferent. The emotions are to be suppressed; pleasure, likewise pain, is a thing of naught. These convictions made the fortress of the Stoic's peace; they also made the sphere of his freedom, where no fear might enter, nor tribulation disturb. Within this sphere of freedom, the lure of pleasures and the shackles of tyrants were alike irrelevant. Such convictions were not merely highminded figments of the Stoic imagination, but even formed the Stoic practice. Yet in time, the famous Stoic *apathy* was replaced by self-mastery and obedience to the will of reason, amid pains and pleasures. These likewise were raised from the class of things indifferent to that of things preferential. And all the while the Stoic, from his recognition of the unity of the world and the oneness of its purpose, perceived the common brotherhood of man, and gained a wider peace in virtuous civic conduct.

This was one sign of the coming time. Another was the strong religiousness with which the Stoic soul turned to the central source of virtue, the personification of all-ruling law — God. This fervour finds a voice in the devout hymn to Zeus by Cleanthes, Zeno's successor, wherein the Stoic heart has personified the all-permeating power so that it may have some One to adore. This hymn seems as a tentative bridge across the abysmal contrast between Aristotle's conception of the Unmoved Mover sunk in self-contemplation, and the God of the coming time, to whom men should pray with new devotion, and in love of whom they should win their adjustment and fulfil their lives. Yet one may deem that there was no such great chasm between the new-found living and loving God, and the God of Plato's *Laws*.

In the meanwhile, if the tide of Stoic devotion overflowed its logic, there was its sister of the Garden, whose gods were undisturbed either by their own beneficence or the prayers of men. Epicurus was Zeno's younger contemporary. Both of them were intent upon living in accord with nature (κατὰ φύσιν) or reason; but while Zeno interpreted this to mean κατ᾽ ἀρετήν, or virtuously, Epicurus said it meant καθ᾽ ἡδονήν, or pleasurably. Epicurus deemed that he had found, as well as Zeno, the peace and quiet of the mind. For he held that the dissipation of pain and anxiety insured happiness,

N

and that the pleasures of the mind were surer and more lasting than sense-joys. As for knowledge, he made no pretence of caring for more of it than would assure the votary of mental ease that his calm should be undisturbed. Philosophy was but a help to happiness. In order to provide a sufficiency of conviction, it should afford a test of truth. So Epicurus recognised sensation as the canon of reality for man. Beyond that, the remembered and multifariously combined images of previous sense-perceptions make the substance of thought; whatever thus presents itself effectively in consciousness is real. For a philosophy of being, he took the atomic theory of Democritus, with its universe constituted by the flux of atoms, and the soul of man made of the very finest. The gods, part of the cosmos, exist in bliss and never interfere. He saw no ground for any other conviction than that pleasure and pain were the absolute good and bad for man. His temperament dwelt more on mental pleasures than on bodily, and tended to set chief store upon a state of divine calm, utterly free from want. To this end, he wisely recognised how small and trifling were the body's needs. And the pleasure of his undisturbed and fearless repose was as much the fruit of will and reason as the Stoic virtue. Virtue also was desirable because pleasant; while friendship, compassion, gentleness were among the loveliest joys of life. Thus for himself and many followers he won freedom and peace of mind. But his creed offered no bulwark against the lower frailties of men — among whom at least it fostered suavity.

So we have sketched the adjustment with life offered by the love of knowledge and exercise of reason in the minds of Greek philosophers. Beginning in the contentment springing from investigation and thought upon the world's origin and laws, this adjustment rose, with Plato and Aristotle, to the sublimest satisfaction of consummate intellectual appetition. But thereupon it narrowed to direct desire for peace of soul, which perhaps is won more surely through employing to their full the highest energies of the mind.

CHAPTER VIII

Intermediaries

WE are considering the striking modes in which great men have adjusted their hopes with what seemed to them the possibilities of their lives; and if we have to touch on less salient ways of adjustment, we may treat them as introductory to those which appear more important in the economy of spiritual progress. In some way, for good or ill, each period of history prepares for that which follows; and great men stand on the shoulders of the great before them — only they need sturdy shoulders for their feet. Heracleitos and his opposite, Parmenides, each lent a shoulder to Plato, affording him a vantage ground needful for his vision, which had been cleared by the dialectic of his master Socrates. And now still looking from the standpoint of adjustment, we may proceed selectively and treat all that follows after Plato and Aristotle, and Zeno and Epicurus, as intermediate and even mediating adjustments making for the acceptance, if not for the origin, of Christianity. If the Hebrew prophets were Christ's truest forerunners, and Jewish formalism his fulcrum of repulsion, later Hellenism, moved and modified by Eastern influences, formed the milieu in which his Gospel was transplanted after his death; a milieu which both contributed to the conquering faith and shaped it to the limitations of this milieu's own receptiveness. Accordingly, one may truly say that from the second century before Christ, the course of Hellenic thought and mood, the intermingling of Eastern religious influences, and the consequent changes occurring in Roman and Greek paganism, all made for the acceptance of that supreme adjustment which was Christianity.

And indeed adjustment was what the world was seeking — adjustment, nay, rather, assurance, and indeed salvation. Even intellectual men no longer found their adjustment in rational investigation, in θεωρία; but were seeking some spiritual stay beyond their reason. Such men, as well as the less intellectual and more emotional millions, now looked to the assurances of religion, in order to free themselves from anxiousness, and gain salvation. Moreover, commonly having found their own opinions insufficient and their ancestral beliefs unsatisfying, they were catching at whatever seemed likely to afford assurance. Men were stirred to a new religious receptiveness and were stimulated morally. Under these conditions, the sharp edges of opinion were relaxed, and opposing systems borrowed from each other. Cults travelled from the Eastern to the

Western boundaries of the Empire, gathering new elements along the way, and themselves gathered in as new elements of old beliefs. Heterogeneous religions formed fruitful unions, while a none too happy give and take seemed to pervade the world.

All this represented need; and the most real answer was the Gospel of Christ, and its preaching and ministration. Let us follow for a little these changes, this loss of intellectual self-reliance, this consequent yielding of thought, this mingling of currents and more ready acceptance of novel opinions and strange beliefs. To start from a concrete example — Stoicism. It began, and for a while continued, as a self-reliant adjustment. Then it softened. By admitting the decent comforts of life as desirable, it relaxed the strictness of its main ethical principle, that the virtuous action of a rationally self-directing will is man's only good. It also humanised its philosophic theology by recognising the people's very human gods. Since the world was full of divine force, why not accept these gods as its personifications? And why not also pertinently accept the Oracles and divination and astrology? Symbolism, allegory, and plastic *etymologies* for the divine names, made ready helps to this desired end — the stoical intelligence thus devising the means and method of believing in accordance with prevailing human needs. Such arguments were applicable, when there was call, to Egypt's gods and Syria's, as well as those of Greece.

The Syrian-born Greek, Poseidonius (cir. 135 to cir. 51 B.C.), pupil of the Rhodian Panætius, embodied the change coming over Stoicism. After his master's death, he left Rhodes, his adoptive home, and travelled far, visiting Egypt, Nubia, Spain, Gaul, and Italy. In all these countries, he studied and investigated, and also saw his great contemporaries, meeting Marius (!) in Rome, and later having Cicero for an auditor at Rhodes. In the universality of his knowledge he seemed a child of Aristotle. None the less was he a child of Plato, of the aged Plato so very absorbent of Pythagoreanism. He was a man of religious feeling and catholic tolerance, even of catholic receptivity; and was much given to those direct and unreasoning modes of realising the divine, and thereby gaining life, which are called mystic. For his philosophy and working religion, he mustered the resources of astronomy, geography, history, astrology, demonology, divination, everything that might enlarge the intellect and assure the mood of man. His knowledge was broad, his reasoning loose, and his constructive faculties were equal to the demands of his ethical and religious enthusiasms. A great and typical figure, he was the protagonist of the spiritual revolution taking place throughout the world of Hellenic thought, and was representative of the tendencies afterwards to culminate in Neoplatonism.[1]

We have now to do with the oriental religions which seem to project themselves into the Hellenic and also the Latin world. They represent ways of thinking and feeling — religious adjustments — accepted in Asia Minor, Syria, and Egypt, lands tinged with Hellenism. We have then to consider the Hellenism penetrating the East, but whose home was in the Greek cities and the Greek lands, a Hellenism which had become as productive, or receptive, of religions as it was of systems of philosophic adjustment. All these adjustments, of oriental cult and Greek orientalised philosophy, will be seen, through a congeniality in need and mood and principles, to prepare men's minds for the Christian deliverance.

There had always been some exchange of blows, and wares, and ideas between the Greeks and the non-Hellenic Mediterranean civilisations. But, of course, with the opportunities and exigencies arising through Alexander's conquest, Hellenic energy cast itself with a new power upon Asia Minor and Persia and Syria and Egypt. Under Alexander's successors, and finally under the Romans, political and social conditions never ceased to further an inter-

[1] On Poseidonius, see *Christ-Schmid, Ges. der Griech. Lit.*, 5th Ed. II, pp. 268 *sqq.*, and compare P. Wendland, *Hellenistisch-Römisch Kultur*, 2d Ed., pp. 134 *sqq.*

change of ideas, and expose Greek and Syrian and
Egyptian to the influence of each other's moods and
thoughts. Lest one should be surprised at the
effect of the East upon Hellenism, and then upon the
Roman West, one should remember that, at least
in Roman times, Syria and Egypt surpassed Greece
and Italy in fertility and wealth and civilization.

Whatever came from the East was in answer to
the cravings or susceptibilities of the West — of
the Greek and Roman world. In the third and
second centuries before Christ, there was still a vast
amount of science and erudition at Alexandria and
other centres of Hellenic culture. And, in Italy,
Rome was at the height of her republican energy.
Nevertheless, under the strain of the last dragging
years of the second Punic war, the Senate (B.C. 205)
decreed the honoured reception of Cybele, the
Phrygian Great Mother, — which was as if a dour
Presbyterian synod in our own time should make a
place for Mother Eddy and her Christian Science in
the Westminster catechism. Likewise from the
close of the second century, the wide-spread and so
largely expatriated Hellenic peoples were yielding
to the religious impulse which was supplanting their
self-reliance. A widely pertinent illustration may
be given of this change of mood. As the satisfying
power of reason weakened, the goddess Tyche [1] —
Chance, blind Fortune — threatened the supremacy

[1] Cf. Rohde, *Der griechische Roman*, pp. 276–282.

of the divine universal law in the world's affairs. She was not reasonable; nor could the rational human will find satisfaction in acquiescing in blind happenings toward which an attitude of voluntary obedience was absurd. And this Tyche-Fortune was worse than blind; she seemed malignant. At all events, with the extension of this wilful Power, the conception of Evil developed as an independent principle hostile to the Good — a conception foreign to classical Greek thought.

Inasmuch as the human will could not render obedience either to Tyche or to the principle of Evil, men were spurred to seek protection against these irresponsible or malignant foes to human peace: and so, reason having failed them, they turned to religion with a new appeal, and sought to link it with such philosophy as they still might cherish. Greek religion, whatever else it was, had always been a means of adjustment, a medium of aid between humanity and the divine. This chief function of religion entered and formed a strain in Greek philosophy, passing betimes from the Orphic mysteries to the system of Pythagoras, and then on into the thought or mood of Plato. It became negation in Epicureanism, since in that system man needed only to assure himself of the indifference of the gods. In Stoicism it was positive, earnest, austere. Even the Scepticism of the later Academy cast sheep's eyes on it.

Outside of such self-respecting and unorientalised systems, the endeavour of the man, thinker or votary, to adjust himself with the divine and gain its support was more unrestrained. It was driven by the desire for unendangered happiness, the yearning for salvation. But as the Roman religion, in the strain of the Punic wars, had failed to satisfy, so generally Hellenic men and women were looking for fuller satisfaction and more responsive aid than their ancestral worship afforded. The oriental cults gave the emotional satisfaction so widely craved. They appealed to the senses and the sentiments, and offered their elaborate symbolism to beguile the minds of the intelligent. They might demand strenuous purification of their votaries, for which they prescribed the method. They also brought the promise of immortality. Wherever accepted, at first casually or by a few, they worked upon the tempers of their votaries, and their diffusion was facilitated through this inclining of men's minds. So the gods and goddesses, and their cults, seemed to gain in power and vogue within the Eastern lands, where they drew adherents from among the Greek strains of population, as at Antioch or Alexandria. Then they advanced beyond those borders to invade the Greek and Latin West. From Phrygia came the Great Mother, Cybele of many forms and names; Attis with her, and his orgiastic rites of mutilation, death, and resurrection; then

from Egypt, Isis, Osiris, Serapis; then many gods
from Syria, tending to transmute themselves to
solar manifestations of universal godhead; lastly
and most potently out of Persia, Mithra the militant, to be recognized by Diocletian as protector
of the Empire[1]; and behind or through them all,
astrology and magic, veritable faiths that alluringly
taught a divine astral fatalism with ways of pro-
pitiating its decrees.

The acceptance of these cults by Greeks and
Romans was not a matter of haphazard chance,
although the motley religious aspect of the later
pagan Empire might lead one to think so. It was
affected by their suitability. For example, the
Greeks of Alexandria, and other Greeks or Romans
following suit, adopted only those Egyptian cults
(of the Osirian circle) which had become half-
Hellenised through Greek influence; they were
syncretistic, exceptionally plastic, and adaptable to
the thoughts and moods of their new votaries. On
the other hand, Mithraism, half-Persian in origin,
and inspired by a strenuous dualism, never touched
the Greeks. Essentially a soldier's faith, and
adapted to militant imperial needs, it passed directly
to the Latin world, which it subdued with power.
All these faiths were offered to their Greek and

[1] See generally, Cumont, *Les Religions orientales dans le Pagan-
isme romain* (1905). There is an English translation and a
second edition.

Latin converts under the guise of "mysteries" accessible only to the duly instructed and initiated, a mode of religious propagation familiar to Greeks and Romans. Their object was union with the god, attained by the priest in ecstasy, and revealed to the votaries. These "mysteries" were secret, as the name implies; they brought intuition, vision, even fruition of the divine. In the initiated, there took place an ecstatic passing away of self, and a rebirth through which the virtues of the god were acquired — his spirit, his power, his immortality. But Osiris, Attis, or Adonis, with whom the devotee was united, had been men, had suffered death, and had risen as gods. Through their mysteries, what they had undergone is not merely learned or seen by the votary, but is veritably experienced and made his own; he is reborn and metamorphosed into the god.

So these religions provided scope for religious passion, and suggested measureless means, both ascetic and voluptuous, for satisfying it. They were direct and personal in their power of assurance, requiring no intervention of state functionaries or promptings of state interests, of which they might indeed be careless. They tended to regroup society according to religious affinities and ties; no more Greeks or Romans, bond or free, but all equal in the mysteries of the Great Mother, of Serapis or Isis. They also brought sure means of purification, and promised a happy immortality.

So they worked a change in Greek, and more markedly (because of its deeply contrasting qualities) in Latin paganism, took the backbone from the latter, broke its rigidity of temper, rendered it fluid, yielding, open to any suggestion or assurance of that salvation which men were craving. And in this religious flux, with its loose assimilation of god and god, goddess and goddess, and their manifestations concrete or symbolical, the more lofty-minded votary could readily think of one god supreme and universal, operative or manifested in many divine forms; he could also purify his faith, and form a synthesis of moral precept agreeing with his gifts. Thus he might harmonise the assurance gained from religion with the adjustment of his moral reason.

From the oriental religions, we turn to certain features of that paganism into which they were passing and were to some extent transforming. It was a Greco-Roman paganism; primarily, of course, Greek in thought, with deflections combined with moral stiffening due to the Roman temperament. Indeed, for our present purpose, the tale begins with those temperamental modifications of Hellenic philosophies, which were worked out by Hellenically educated Romans who retained the strength of their Roman natures. It leads on through later phases of a paganism wherein Roman qualities are scarcely distinguishable in the Hellenic-oriental blend, out of which will

then be seen to issue that last great pagan philo-
sophic-religious adjustment of man to the god within
him and without, which we call Neoplatonism.

Let us notice certain Roman very personal re-
adjustments of Hellenic attitudes toward life.
Looking to the days of the Republic, we are impressed by the almost portentous figure of Lucretius,
— a great talent, an austere and powerful temperament. Who does not at least know of his poem
De natura rerum, in which he invoked Lady Venus
and hailed pleasure as Life's Leader — "Dux vitæ
dia voluptas." But the poem was written to release
himself and other mortals from the anxieties and
ills that men had made for themselves out of
their vain fear of the gods. Relief from fear, reliance
on reason, and acquiescence in the knowledge of
the nature of things, which reason had won, made
the adjustment of this man, whose hatred of
religion, uniting with Roman austerity, chose to
reset the Stoic temper and ethical ideal in the
Epicurean scheme of physics and theology.

As of course, in the great days of the Republic,
the individual Roman citizen, somewhat inarticu-
lately and unconsciously, had merged himself in the
fortunes of his country. Largely speaking, that was
his devotion, and that was his adjustment; his fortunes stood with hers; and he felt his own life
carried on in the lives of his children, themselves
again making part of the all-enveloping *respublica*.

Both he and the Republic were scrupulous in their religious observances, that they might not err and lose the favour of the gods. In all of this, we may think the Romans self-taught, instructed by their temper and their exigencies; yet any part of this Roman adjustment might have been learned from Sparta, or from the great days of Athens.

Likewise one sees that the ideal Vergilian adjustment is the Augustan or imperial. The great pagan heart of the supreme Roman poet knew the sorrow entailed by endeavour, and felt the pathos of mortal lives. This depth of feeling, this realisation of the sacrifice required, gives truth and power to the lesson of the Æneid, which teaches fulfilment of duty, yea, of destiny, and in obedience to God. The energy of a great epoch was needed to attain this imperial adjustment, valid for the Empire, and perhaps ideally valid for its citizens if only they would be staunch. In fact, it was real and satisfying for but few — perhaps it was too politically inspired. An adjustment coming closer to the individual was needed even by noble natures.

Such a one was Horace, in whose urbanity were mingled the finest flavours of Epicureanism and Stoicism. Kindness, knowledge of men, tolerance of human faults, fondness for pleasure, consciousness of its insufficiency, self-control within his limitations, all contributed to the well-being of this admirably trimmed and balanced nature. He leaned

toward Epicureanism while life's pleasures ran in
their early grooves; but the thoughtfulness of years
and the pathos of mortality drew him — inter-
mittently perhaps — toward a more stable satisfaction. He began to praise virtue, the sterling
Vergilian virtues of old Rome. The thought of
them gave him strength. And while he still felt
that the contented mind, the *aequum animum*, must
rest upon itself, he looked more constantly to God
to support and enrich his life — for which he would
be grateful:

> Tu quamcumque deus tibi fortunaverit horam
> Grata sume manu, neu dulcia differ in annum.

Perhaps he thought it best to seize the sunny
day — *carpe diem!* — even within the providence of
God!

Three men lived under the Empire, belonging to
three generations, in whom Stoicism is clothed and
decent, not given to religious orgies, and yet is
moving with the tendencies of the time toward the
expression of a religious ethics corresponding at
many points with the ethics of patristic Christianity.
Their adjustment with life still rested in reason and
the resolutely accordant will; and yet their still
rational adjustment was becoming prayerful, seeking some assurance from God. No need to say that
these men were Seneca, Epictetus, and Marcus
Aurelius.

o

The finished Stoical aphorisms of the first do not inspire complete confidence. One doubts whether the frail disposition of man could live up to anything so perfect. A mind despising the accidents of fortune, and happy in virtue, is the *summum bonum*, and constitutes the human adjustment with Seneca. Accordingly, no evil can come to a good man; misfortune is his opportunity,— and many more like cheering utterances. Yet Seneca made the conventional Stoical concessions to the weakness of human nature — one prefers to have joys to moderate, rather than griefs to repress. The sage is not a stone: how could virtue be virtue unless it felt its trials. He also recognised social duties, which had long been part of virtue. And he was religious: in regno nati sumus; deo parere libertas est, — Obedience to God, that is our liberty. Seneca's god is the perfect and stern Stoic sage, having no weaknesses, and recognising none! There is friendship, as there is likeness, between God and good men, for whom he reserves his disciplinary benevolence, while he lets the wicked wanton in their lusts. He tries the good man with adversity, and delights to watch the struggle. Neither God, nor the Stoic sage, sorrows over human misfortune; but views all life through the eyes of the Stoic reason.

Epictetus was not so rich as Seneca, and his life rings truer to his principles. He thinks more constantly of God; philosophy has become religion with him. He can be thankful to God not only for the vine and wheat, but for the virtuous mind, which is indeed a part of God, who has set the law that man's good shall lie in his rational will, invincible from without, even by God. But let man reflect always on God and the divine providence in the world; let him attempt nothing without God. The true philosopher will "know that he is sent a messenger from Zeus to men about good and bad things, to show them that they have wandered and are seeking the substance of good and evil where it is not." [1]

Born a slave and made a freedman, Epictetus was a contented man, his happiness established in his reason and his will, and warmed with entire trust in God. But Marcus was a different kind of pagan saint. He was burdened with the rule of an Empire, a thankless, hopeless task filling him with intellectual melancholy. His philosophy, his religion, was essentially the same as that of Epictetus. His palace was to him as the freedman's cottage; for he needed as few things as Epictetus. Indeed he might have been happier in a lowly station, which would have left him untried and undisciplined by such harassing responsibilities. Marcus is disposed to pray to the gods even for things within his own power, for freedom from anxiety and fear and grief, as well as

[1] Dis. III, 22. Long's translation.

from vain desires.   Though strong in his reason and Stoic virtue, he felt the need of aid.

"Follow God and love mankind," says Marcus, for love of one's neighbour is a property of the rational soul, conscious of its affinity to other souls and God. Satisfaction lies in always acting thus — obediently and in accordance with right reason.   All is prepared from eternity — the thread of thy being, along with other things!   The Universe loves whatever is to be; and as it loves, so love I.   Yet in Marcus this philosophic satisfaction might become mere resignation.   He was a little weary of the universe he loved.   He feared his imagination, was distrustful of his heart, or at least felt the need to steel it through meditation on mortality as an incident in the universal necessity of dissolution.   If his soul was not embittered, still the whole whirl and flux of life seemed but a pointless warfare, from which, when released, he would depart satisfied.

Stoicism is tired in Marcus; it no longer cheers. It has depressed the human heart; it has shut its eyes too resolutely against feelings which it could not entertain, against hopes which it could not justify. Stoicism could not really approve of love, which is longing and anxiety and rapture, and not unmoved benevolence.   In fine, the Stoic God could not love, the Stoic physics admitted no immortality.   The age demanded both, and Stoicism became a discarded creed.

The treatises of Seneca and the *Discourses* of Epictetus survive as illustrious examples of the philosophic propaganda and ethical exhortation current in the first and second centuries of what was scarcely yet the Christian era. Many austere figures moved through the Empire, endeavouring to recall men from their folly to a truer realisation of their nature, and instructing them how they might be saved from the evil of the world. This preaching drew from the moral stores of the Hellenistic philosophies, which were becoming religious faiths. It sought to cast men on their inner selves, upon their spiritual lives, and point out how their true and enduring natures might be rescued and *saved*. It taught higher thoughts of God, and the yielding oneself to the divine will as the truest sacrifice. In life as well as doctrine, these men had much in common with the life and message of those who were preaching Christianity. Yet the fullest approximation to contemporary Christianity, and the most efficient influence upon human moods making for its acceptance, was that final Hellenistic system of philosophy and religion, called Neoplatonism, which also offered men the adjustment, or perhaps deliverance, nearest to the salvation offered by the Christian faith.

There were apparently abysms of difference between Stoicism and Neoplatonism. Yet the philosophic and pietistic eclecticism of the latter had its antecedent in the eclectically expanded Stoicism of Poseidonius; though, to be sure, the system of which he was the nominal adherent seems again to contract its phylacteries in Seneca and Marcus. That may be referred, however, to their personal tempers, rather than to any tendency of their time.

Neoplatonism was the creature of mood and metaphysics. It united metaphysics and ethics with religious ecstasy. Plotinus, who died in the year 270 A.D., was its constructor. He was a metaphysical genius and also a man so austere in spirit that it cost him little effort to ignore the body's needs. He drew upon the previous great systems of Greek thought, — upon Aristotle, upon Stoicism, above all upon Plato. But while he was a master-builder with their reasonings, he had no aptitude for physical science. Hence his philosophy royally neglected the accumulated scientific knowledge of the past, and thus fell in with the tendencies of its time. In part, Plotinus's system was a last result of Plato's idealism. But with this metaphysical Egyptian, far more fatuously than with the great Athenian master of knowledge as well as dialectic, the aspirations of the soul became the criterion, and the sum, of human knowledge.

To attain its ends, Neoplatonism made use of means which would have been abominations to the purer Greek philosophies. It wantoned in allegory, and in that way explained and justified any foolish-

ness to which its followers felt drawn. From the
beginning it was touched with the Orient; and then
quickly embraced those motley cults and superstitions in which the Orient had the greater part.
Even Plotinus was driven by a yearning to be saved
from the confusion of mortal life. His aim was
neither knowledge nor the satisfaction springing
from the ultimate consideration of facts and values,
which is philosophy. His mind was filled with the
desire of ecstatic spiritual well-being, which his
reason could neither attain nor justify. The goal he
looked to was supra-rational ecstatic union with the
Absolute One.

To be sure, this goal was led up to through the
discipline of ethics and long lines of metaphysical
prolegomena, — with Plotinus. His disciple Porphyry still liked to reason, and had that faculty;
but his temper was distraught, and religious anxiousness drove him to questionable spiritual drugs.
He was incredulous as to demons — how can they
harm a pure soul? But his imagination, like the
age he lived in, swarmed with them. He talks of
them continually, as did Tertullian, and the great
Origen, and that doughty pagan, Celsus, against
whom Origen wrote. The age was obsessed with
demons. It were best to take them without qualms
and cheerfully, as Plutarch had done, and as Iambli-
cus, the Neoplatonic hierophant who followed
Porphyry, was to do. With him Neoplatonism

casts off restraint, flings wide its arms to every superstition, and endeavours on principle to justify belief in the incredible and reliance upon the absurd — upon theurgy with all its magic words and acts. Thenceforth it kept open house for all phases of popular paganism. Yet its more intellectual adherents might still attach themselves to its metaphysics, its system of emanation of life and being from the One to the Nous, and from the Nous to the World-soul and the souls of men.

In its strenuous and more consistent phases, Neoplatonism was ascetic. For, pushing on along the dualistic currents of the time, it had come to discredit matter for its lack of metaphysical reality, and hate it for its defilements of the flesh-entangled soul, the lures with which it stopped the soul's progress toward ecstatic union with the All-spirit, the All-real, the All-One.

Obviously, even with its metaphysical inceptor, Neoplatonism, rising above human reason, yearning for salvation from material unrealities, looking toward union with the Ineffable, demanded the immediate support of that toward which the soul was reaching as the goal of bliss, and which by itself the soul could not attain. The Divine draws on the ardent philosopher by its own perfect Being: it awaits the upward striving soul. But how when the soul is blind and feeble? Will not the Divine in some way meet the soul, reveal Itself, and hold out aid ? Can It not be induced to aid ? Are there not mediatorial means ? The soul of Plotinus was strong with spiritual impulse; the souls of others after him required stimulus and aid and guidance. They called for a lowering of the mediatorial means, and looked for plain and palpable modes of revelation. Neoplatonism became whatever its votaries required. It took what they wished from Egypt, accepted the Sun and planetary worship from Syria; it filled itself out with divination and astrology. Accepting the ritual and method of the Eastern mysteries, it developed means of mediation, educated a priesthood skilled in magic, able to win the god's aid and reveal his will; able likewise to defend the votary from the myriad demons which beset men everywhere, benumbing, frightening, or distracting the worshipper, even thronging the temples, and requiring dispersal before the true god can appear. Neoplatonism represents the last and most inclusive blending of Hellenic-oriental elements in a final paganism, a final pagan religion, having its reason and unreason, its decencies and indecencies, suited to the motley multitude of its votaries.

From our point of view it was the last Hellenic adjustment — an adjustment quickly overflowing reason, seeking assurance and salvation from without, becoming a religion. Plotinus, incredulous of matter, pressed toward ecstasy and union with the One, through his own reason and his own spiritual energy.   That was his adjustment, — an adjustment needing little assurance beyond the power of its impulse.   But Porphyry, his disciple, already fearful, is all too conscious of the waverings of his soul, its hankerings after all manner of indecorous enchantments which his reason could not quite effectively contemn.   For his adjustment, he needed magic nostrums as well as the deeper assurances of faith. And after Porphyry, though some men might have rational thoughts, none drew back from whatever spiritual comfort might be suggested by fancy or current superstition.   For ten that yearned for union with the One, thousands sought the stay and strength, the protection, power, even the immortal nature, of whatever god into whose "mysteries" they were initiated.

Contemporaries, though they may disavow and anathematise each other, have nearly everything in common except perhaps the specific points on which they think they differ. Gnostics, Neoplatonists, Manichæans, Arians, Catholic Christians of the third and fourth centuries, had indefinitely more in common than we can have with any of them, whatever be our sympathies. Yet on the other hand, the fuller our knowledge becomes of the manifold likenesses between Christianity and all the other religions swarming in those centuries, the more surely we are driven to the recognition of dynamic qualities in Catholic Christianity by which

it emerged victorious from the maze of contemporary systems, even though it never freed itself
from the current views and superstitions of the age
which accepted and partly fashioned it.

One may safely emphasise the likenesses between
Neoplatonism and Christianity, in practical morality, in occasional asceticism, in religious anxiousness (especially concerning the besetting hosts of
devils), in the conscious need of saving mediation,
and generally in credulity and receptive mood. The
spiritual needs of Neoplatonists and Christians were
similar, though the two religions had very different
means of satisfying them.

One may say much the same of the Gnostic
systems, a group of religious phenomena taking
their rise before the Christian era, but afterwards
acquiring more striking features and enormous
vogue. Gnosticism carried a mixture of oriental
and Hellenic elements, and tended to become a
sort of bastard Christianity. It was by no means
unrelated to Neoplatonism, since it strove to intuit
and behold its god, and so unite with him and gain
his strength; it even sought to effect such union
through veritable experience of the divine, the
supernatural or supermaterial. The Gnostic union
with the Divine might take place in passionate
sense modes. Gnosticism was also dualistic, finding
everywhere the action of good and evil. Indeed its
various systems seem almost to arise out of this

problem of the origin of evil. Of course, the Gnostic religions were full of demons, and erudite with spells to drive them from the soul journeying on to its salvation. Salvation was its aim; and that drew it to Christianity. But the Gnostic salvation had been a weird and mystic process entwined with man's origin, rather than conceived as springing from a definite historical event. Gnosticism would adopt the Christian Saviour: but diverse and grotesque were the struggles of its sects to make the Saviour into an element of their belief; for no Gnostic sect could accept him in the reality of his manhood, or admit that the Saviour died upon the cross.

The struggle of Gnosticism to become Christian, or to make Christianity Gnostic, was the supreme peril of early Christianity wherein it was in danger of becoming a hybrid. But it gained strength from its resistance, and greater definitude of creed; thereby, at the same time, proving itself a living thing, an organic faith, that could not blend with another system.

So Catholic Christianity became itself more clearly through this miraculous process of pulling itself out of the swirl which surrounded and almost seemed to have cradled it. In this it clung to its adjustment, of Christ, and in Christ and the Church; and this clinging to its adjustment, its assurance, its salvation, was at the same time, necessarily, a rejection of the similar or dissimilar adjustments, the insufficient assurances and revelations, the vague mediatorial means, and the unreal, the fantastic, the unhuman and undivine salvations, which were not its own.

Arianism and Manichæism were the last two systems, so like and yet so fatally unlike Catholic Christianity, which it had to disclaim, or from which it had to free itself. The former was a Christian heresy, filled in its time with the possibilities of all kinds of dogmatic idolatry — not merely the harmless genial worship of the saints, which Catholic Christianity held to. If Gnosticism had impugned the reality of Christ's manhood, Arianism impugned the reality of his godhead. But Catholic Christianity was to cling to this dual reality as the sufficient mediatorial means of salvation.

More from without, and yet with many dangerous likenesses, was Manichæism, — from which our final example of deliverance, Augustine, will be seen to drag himself with pain. It was a drastic dualism, sprung mainly from Persian Magianism, but absorbing also Christian matter, and making a particularly malignant and pessimistic blend. Nor was this tare ever rooted out; for as the rankest of heresies it clung to the skirts of Christianity through the Middle Ages.

Fingit sibi quisque colendum, mens vaga quod suadet.[1]

Setting these words of some Latin poet as the epitaph of these oriental pagan systems, we shall

[1] From Rohde, *Griechischer Roman*, 2d Ed., p. 19.

now turn to Christianity, whose man-god was not
fashioned by the rambling mind. In that there was
not only reality, but reality manifold if not inconsist-
ent! Whatever appears real in the others, is somehow absorbed in Catholic Christianity, and raised
to a higher power, — morals, asceticism, needs,
and the means of their satisfaction. It was even a
yoking of opposites, blind faith and rational enlightenment, obedience and disobedience, all according to the spirit. A mighty exercise of mind begins
within the Church, in which these opposites work
together for the building up of the Christian man,
and the making firm of the Christian adjustment,
the Christian assurance, the Christian salvation.

CHAPTER IX

Jesus

THE prudent mind halts before the mystery of Jesus Christ. It will hesitate to attempt to characterise the adjustment with life and God of one from whom proceeded modes of deliverance for mankind. How shall one conceive of the personal assurance of salvation in him who soon was to be held the salvation of the world ? We have the records, and with whatever differences of opinion we may regard them, we should not deliver ourselves over to the sweet conceit of selecting what seems probable, and rejecting what does not. If we suspect the records, or reject them, what other means of information have we touching this being, human or divine, or both, as to whom we must hold some opinion, seeing that he was at least the fountain-head of our religion ? Recent scholarship has gathered and arranged the multifarious array of contemporary resemblances to nearly everything in primitive Christianity, and has set forth the moulding and remoulding influences into which the Gospel of Christ was cast. Nearly every element, even in that first Gospel core, seems to have had its alien counterpart. But even then these alien counterparts were jaded phantasms; while the Gospel was a thing of human and divine reality. Its life made its originality. He who would search into the vital truth of it needs all his scholarship, and yet must not spend himself on husks, or be satisfied with analogies between what is dead and what is living, between the vagaries of the tired imagination, and principles rooted in human, if not divine, verity.

In the main, we must keep to the records, proceeding exegetically, and not building too much from our own modern minds, or our conceptions of what must have been. We can scarcely expect to see into the inscrutable adjustment of Jesus, which rested in his nature and his relationship to God. In the oneness of this adjustment, there is duality. For we shall find no adjustment in the man Jesus, unless we treat him as the Messiah and the Son of God — as he deemed himself. His adjustment cannot be treated as that of a simple man, for in the records he is more than man. It is inseverable from his more than human function as the Saviour of men : it forms part of the Gospel, part of the Kingdom of God, which is the salvation of mankind.

One will also recognise the originality of Jesus, both in his adjustment and in his Gospel to men. He had antecedents, and he moved in an environment from which he drew his fund of incidental knowledge or ignorance as to man and the visible, even the invisible, world. Let us take a striking

example: the men of Jesus' time, and those of the
following centuries, were surrounded by demons;
all life was enveloped with them. The minds
even of the best, Plutarch, Celsus as well as Origen,
all the Church Fathers, are infested with them,
and are disposed to gauge the efficacy of a faith by
its power over demons, the demons of pollution,
the demons of madness, the demons of disease.
Jesus also, just as he preaches and heals the sick, so
with equal potency he casts out demons; he gives
his apostles authority to preach and cast out demons:
κηρύσσειν and ἐκβάλλειν τὰ δαιμόνια go together from
the beginning of his ministry. Thus exorcism
pervades the Gospel, and will pervade the whole
Church through the following centuries. Yet does
it really penetrate to the life of Christ and the Gospel
of Christ? At all events not in any explanatory
manner: for it is incidental and detachable, and
though it was certainly part of the working Gospel
for many years, we know that Christ and his Gospel
were not the fruit of these opinions of the time.
Consideration of such environing or antecedent
beliefs gives but a partial and superficial view of
him. Not by these ways shall we penetrate the
nature of Christ, and enter the sphere of his moving
convictions, which constituted his adjustment, his
relationship with God.

Now, following our records, and perhaps distrustful both of ourselves and them, let us see at all

P

events how we may understand the adjustment wherein Jesus kept his life at one, with peace of mind, and spirit free to do its perfect work. God was his father. Strength, confidence, peace, life, in fine, came from him, and on the Son's part was energised by the single motive of doing the Father's will. The power and compass of this motive was the will of God, his Father, as Jesus realised it within himself and brought the inner realisation to outer actuality in word and act. His dependence was entire; his faith included the perfect faith of a man. His conduct represented the perfect righteousness of man, fulfilling, for example, those unified "Beatitudes" of the "Sermon on the Mount," as well as all the precepts grouped within that "Sermon's" amplitude. It fulfilled whatever Jesus demanded of men.

But many sayings in the Gospels, which apply to him and his relationship to God, and, as it were, disclose features of his adjustment, do not apply to men. One may pass from general precepts binding upon all, to other statements which illumine their significance, and yet relate directly to Christ alone. "Thou shalt love the Lord thy God with all thy heart and with all thy soul and with all thy mind — and thy neighbour as thyself": these two commands, which Jesus more clearly than the ancient writers knew to contain the purport and content of the Law, he lived and dwelt in. "He who seeks to save his life, shall lose it, and he who loseth his life for my sake shall save it": here again Jesus was the incarnate fulfilment of his own words to men.

We turn to other words of his which reflect illumination on the giving up of life for the Gospel's sake, and on the love which men shall have for God, and yet primarily set forth a relationship between the Son and Father which is beyond human participation: "All things have been delivered unto me of my Father: and no one knoweth the Son save the Father; neither doth any know the Father, save the Son, and he to whomsoever the Son willeth to reveal him." The next verses continue: "Come unto me all ye that labour and are heavy laden, and I will give you rest. Take my yoke [*i.e.* my precepts] upon you, and learn of me." Jesus points to himself as the end and goal, just as he speaks of the Kingdom of God as that wherein men reach the relationship to God which is salvation. His love was the Father's love, and his life did the Father's work of love toward men. He demanded faith in himself, in his Christhood, his power from God to save. Consider the sequence of the verses in the eighth chapter of Mark: "If any man would come after me, let him deny himself, and take up his cross, and follow me. For whosoever would save his life shall lose it; and whosoever shall lose his life for my sake and the Gospel's shall save it. For what doth it profit a man, to gain the whole world, and forfeit

his life ?   For what should a man give in exchange
for his life ?   For whosoever shall be ashamed of
me and of my words in this adulterous and sinful
generation, the Son of man also shall be ashamed of
him, when he cometh in the glory of his Father
with the holy angels.   And he said unto them,
Verily I say unto you, there be some here of them
that stand by, which shall in no wise taste of death,
till they see the Kingdom of God come with power." [1]

Thus Jesus discloses his conception of himself.
It was at one with his conviction of his mission to men
and his relationship to God.   "Verily the Son of man
came not to be ministered unto, but to minister and
to give his life a ransom for many."   Often, and under
varied circumstances, Jesus tells his disciples that
he shall be put to death and, on the third day,
rise again.   There is no statement coming from him
so frequently repeated in the Gospels.   It seems
to represent the core of his assurance of his mission,
and the bleeding heart of his faith in God his Father,
— who should bring him to his death and also raise
him up on the third day.   The power of his faith
sees even further — and shall we consider this also
a feature of his personal adjustment or assurance ?
The Son of man shall come in great power and
glory, to judge the world, and send the angels to
gather his elect.   It may be that Jesus drew the
form of his convictions as to his final coming from

[1] Cf. Matt. xvi. 24–28; xxv. 31–46.

Messianic expectations current with his race, even as
he accepted prevalent beliefs as to demoniac possession.   But, again, the borrowed form, so far as it
was borrowed, casts but a surface gleam upon the
moving energies of his faith.

Such seems to me the nature of Jesus' adjustment
of himself with God.   Amplifications will suggest
themselves — indeed they fill the Gospels, or constitute *the* Gospel.   And so far we have kept to the
Synoptics as the more generally accepted record.
The Fourth Gospel seems to issue from a stage of
further reflection upon the earthly life and death
of Jesus, and upon the eternal power and love and
life of Christ.   Thoughts to be held to, thoughts
to be rejected, had pressed upon the writer, arising
or suggested (some of them, perhaps, by Paul
or his Epistles) since the time when Jesus walked on
earth.   But their effect upon the uplifted mind of
this evangelist does not impair the value of his understanding of Christ.   I do not see why our historical
consciousness should be shocked at taking his Gospel
as spiritually complementary to the Synoptics, and
as throwing the light of completion upon such conceptions of Jesus' personal adjustment as they give.
This further and completing adjustment is of the
divine love, which is life and gives life.

"For God so loved the world that he gave his only
begotten son, that everyone believing on him
should not perish, but have eternal life."

"The Father loveth the Son, and hath given all
things into his hand. He that believeth on the
Son, hath eternal life" (iii. 16, 35, 36).

"Even as the Father hath loved me, I also have
loved you; abide ye in my love. If ye keep my
commandments, ye shall abide in my love; even as
I have kept my Father's commandments, and abide
in his love. These things have I spoken unto you,
that my joy may be in you, and that your joy may
be fulfilled."

"This is my commandment that ye love one
another, as I have loved you. Greater love hath
no man than this, that a man give up his life for
his friends" (xv. 9–12, 13).

In these passages, a number of cognate thoughts
tend to unite, to become in and of each other:
God's love for his Son and for the world; the Son
abiding in the Father's love, and sharing in the
Father's love of man; men doing the divine will,
abiding in the divine love, and loving one another.
With the result that they shall be saved and have
eternal life, which is theirs who abide in the love of
God, — the love which wills eternal life and makes to
live. The end is the union of believers, the union of
obedient lovers, in Christ and God. It is evident
that the Son's adjustment with the Father embraces
the salvation of mankind, is even identical with it.

This will appear more clearly if we turn back
and follow the Gospel for a little. "God is spirit,"

Jesus has said to the Samaritan woman; and when his disciples have returned to the well, and ask him to eat, he answers that he has meat they know not of, which is to do the will of him who sent him. After the healing at the Bethesda pool, he says to the Jews, "He that heareth my word, and believeth him that sent me, *hath* eternal life, and cometh not into judgement, but hath passed out of death into life. . . . For as the Father hath life in himself, even so gave he to the Son also to have life in himself. . . . I can do nothing of myself." And at another time: "I am come down from heaven, not to do mine own will, but the will of him that sent me. And this is the will of him that sent me, that of all that which he hath given me, I should lose nothing, but should raise it up at the last day."

Here it is clear, that as Christ's adjustment is to do his Father's will, which is that no believing life shall be lost, so that adjustment must include the imparting of eternal life to all believers. The absolute life-giving power of spirit is next declared. "I am the bread of life," — a hard saying to the Jews. In the explanation to the disciples, Jesus says: "It is the spirit that maketh life": τὸ πνεῦμά ἐστιν τὸ ζωοποιοῦν. Even as it is the *truth* that maketh free, free from the bondage to sin, wherein there cannot be the eternal freedom of the spirit.

" . . . and I lay down my life for the sheep. . . . My sheep hear my voice . . . and I give them eternal life; and they shall never perish, and no one shall snatch them out of my hand. My Father, which hath given them unto me, is greater than all; and no one is able to snatch them out of the Father's hand. I and the Father are one."

The final discourses with the disciples contain the fullest expression of the adjustment of the Son with and in the Father; they also set forth the ultimate phases of that love and life which Christ is, in and of the Father, and which those receive who love him, and thereby become one with him and the Father. They include the fourteenth chapter of John, and then the fifteenth with its image of the true Vine, also the sixteenth, a chapter of love's consolations, — "that in me ye may have peace"; and finally the seventeenth, where analysis may well hesitate.

"Father, the hour is come; glorify thy Son that the Son may glorify thee: even as thou hast given him authority over all flesh, that whatsoever thou hast given him, to them he should give eternal life. And this is life eternal, that they should know thee, the only true God, and him whom thou didst send, even Jesus Christ. I glorified thee on the earth, having accomplished the work which thou hast given me to do. And now, O Father, glorify thou me with thine own self with the glory which I had with thee before the world was."

Thereupon the prayer turns directly to the disciples and those who are to believe through their word: "Sanctify them in the truth; thy word is truth . . . that they may all be one; even as thou, Father, art in me, and I in thee, that they also may be in us: that the world may believe that thou didst send me.   And the glory which thou hast given me I have given unto them; that they may be one, even as we are one; I in them, and thou in me, that they may be perfected into one . . . that the love wherewith thou lovedst me may be in them, and I in them."

So far as the mystery of Christ may be unveiled, these words declare that the adjustment, the assurance, the salvation, which was his and in his life, consummates itself in the life of God and in the salvation of men, through the divine love and the imparting of life through love's sanctifying truth.

CHAPTER X

Paul

PAUL'S antecedents as a Jew and education as a Pharisee drastically shaped the creative working of his religious genius, and set the ways through which he reached that power of conviction which was to move the Gentile world. The intellectual necessities of this Jew and Pharisee, in conflict and in alliance with his experience of Christ, moulded the form of his adjustment, his devotion, and his assurance of salvation. Some of his phrases, even some of his conceptions, may have been taken from the mystery-religions of the Hellenistic world he moved in. When the phrases or the ideas of those ubiquitous cults offered themselves as vehicles for the expression, or means for the clarification, of his thoughts of Christ and his new relationship to God through Christ, he naturally used them.

Leaving his birthplace, the Hellenistic city of Tarsus, Paul went to Jerusalem as a youth, where he diligently studied the law of Israel at the feet of Gamaliel. That honoured Pharisee appears as the most tolerant and patient-minded of his class. It was he who stayed the first persecution of the apostles, warning the Sanhedrin to beware, since

perchance the teaching in the name of Jesus might be
of God (Acts v).   Yet he was a learned master and
strict observer of the law; and there was at least
one zealot in his school.   That zealot, somewhat
later, is found approving of the death of Stephen,
and then becomes an eager persecutor of the followers
of Jesus.   Active at Jerusalem in committing them
to prison, he takes letters from the High Priest to
the Damascus synagogues, in order that he may hunt
them there.

Although Saul's persecution of the Church is
frequently referred to in the Acts and in his own
Epistles, we are not intimately informed as to its
motives, save that it sprang from zeal for the law:
"Ye have heard," he writes to the Galatians, "of
my manner of life in time past in the Jews' religion,
how that beyond measure I persecuted the Church of
God, and made havoc of it: and I advanced in the
Jews' religion beyond many of mine companions
among my countrymen, being more exceedingly
zealous for the traditions of my fathers."

So we cannot tell just what was working in the
mind of the young man Saul, while the garments of
those who were stoning Stephen were in keeping
at his feet; nor what was surging in him while on
the way to Damascus.   Zealous for the law, was he
wilfully hurrying on, lest he find himself stopped by
the reluctance of misgivings and the dissuasion of
counter impulses ?   Such matters, and the more

definite stroke of illumination and repentance which overcame him, each of us will interpret for himself: the resources of modern psychology are at our disposal. That "vision," however, was to be an uplifting — not an overturning — of the contents of Paul's education and convictions.

After he was led into the city, and his sight had been restored by brother Ananias, or, as he puts it in his own words, looking back after many years' consideration: "when it was the good pleasure of God, who separated me, even from my mother's womb, and called me through his grace, to reveal his Son in me, that I might preach him among the Gentiles, *straightway I did not take counsel with flesh and blood . . . but I went away into Arabia*" (Gal. i).

We are ignorant of the nature and setting of this retirement. Let us not imagine that we can think as Paul; his very words, impressed with his experience and peculiar education, do not bear the same meaning to us that they had for him. We must not be too sure that we really understand the argumentation of his Epistles; still less can we penetrate the conflicts, or the reasonings within himself, which we think he must have passed through, before he attained to those convictions and that power of faith which were to move the Gentiles. But at least we must interpret this journey into Arabia as a period of retirement and reflection. It is inconceivable that he did not need a time of quiet to restore his mind, and enable him to get new bearings on the old sea of his fathomless education and inheritance, before he could steer a course by the light flashing within him.

As to arguments and communings with himself, before his great convictions came, we can only work back to them very uncertainly, by inference. And yet it seems as if we could trace, for instance, in a writing of such personal intensity as the Epistle to the Galatians, something of the process by which those convictions had become a very part of Paul, belonging to his mental and religious growth, as we might say, or, as he would deem, springing from the power of Christ within him.

But before making this approach to a view of the scope and contents of the great deliverance which Paul attained in Christ, its basis, as it were the body which was to be transformed and clothed upon, must be grasped. Paul was a Jew, and to the end remained a Jew, faithful to the God of his fathers, and faithful to the law of Israel as he conceived that law to have been fulfilled in Christ. If Jesus said that not one jot or tittle of the law should pass away till all things were fulfilled, so Paul, following the argumentation in which he had been trained, and holding fast to the law's elemental or pedagogic authority, rises above it through its own reasonings, compels the old to support the new, and so fulfil

itself in Christ. "Do we then make the law of none
effect through faith? Nay, we establish the law" —
even in the principle of justification through faith.
Is not this a large part of the burden of the Epistle to
the Romans? A burden which is carried with
strainings of the spirit! The bearer is driven forward by the sense of his own inability to fulfil the
law, — a deep and dreadful sense of his radically
evil nature, which compels him to do the thing he
hates. This body of sin and death must literally
be *dispossessed* and replaced by the spirit of Christ,
which we have through faith and hope and love.

It is wonderful how legal are Paul's arguments,
and through what tortuous and narrow-necked passages he emerges into the breadth of the truth of
Christ. It is all there in *Romans:* the twistings
seem to end with the seventh chapter, and with
the opening of the eighth, Paul has cast off the
body of this death and freed himself from the condemnation of the law: "There is therefore no
condemnation to them that are in Christ Jesus . . .
and we know that to them that love God all things
work together for good. . . ." And yet, perhaps
alas! perhaps unavoidably, Paul must needs re-
trammel himself in arguments touching the righteousness of God's foreordainment as to the elect.
Because of such hamperings and hindrances, Paul,
with all his splendid breadth and truth of mind
and heart, perhaps seems to fail to dwell quite

easily in the absolute universality of the Fatherhood
of God and the spirit of Christ, life-giving, re-
creating. Yet with fervent power he makes even
that his own, through revelation and the grace of
God.

It will now be illuminating to follow the argument
of the Epistle to the Galatians. The fervour of
his exhortations to those people, well-meaning, and
yet foolish and bewitched, harks back to disputa-
tions with himself, in the years when he had need
to press his way through each successive difficulty
springing out of his education — thorns for his feet!
We feel the admonition of the superscription:
"Paul an apostle, *not from men!* . . . grace to you
and peace from God the Father, and our Lord
Jesus Christ, who gave himself for our sins, that
he might deliver us out of this present evil world."
The admonition becomes explicit in the next sentences. Then he recalls how he had made known to
them that the Gospel which he preached came to him
through revelation of Jesus Christ, not from the
instruction of James, Cephas, or John, who, nevertheless, in good time gave him the right hand of
fellowship, as having been intrusted with the Gospel
for the Gentiles. And he recounts that subsequent
argument with Cephas, in which he so energetically
bade him to remember that even he, Cephas, did not
live like a Jew, but believed in Christ in order to be
justified through faith in Christ, and not by works

of the law; since by works of the law shall no flesh
be justified.

Then he turns and demands of them: "Received
ye the Spirit by the works of the law, or by the hearing of the faith ?   Are ye so foolish ? having begun
in the Spirit, are ye now perfected in the *flesh?*"
May not Paul have pricked himself with this same
sarcasm, and often asked himself these very questions, while he was adjusting his past with the call
through grace and the revelation of the Son in him,
which first took place on a certain day when on
the road to Damascus ? Some twenty years had
passed since then. And now he quotes to his
Galatians those words from the fifteenth chapter of
Genesis, which seem never to have left his mind —
repeatedly he quotes them, and how often must he
have said them to himself: "Abraham believed God,
and it was reckoned unto him for righteousness."
He draws for his hearers the inference, with which
doubtless he often had assured himself, that he still
was an inheritor of the promise made to Abraham:
"Know therefore that they which be of faith, the
same are sons of Abraham. And the Scripture,
foreseeing that God would justify the Gentiles
by faith, preached the Gospel beforehand unto
Abraham, saying, In thee shall all the nations be
blessed." So then they which be of faith are blessed
with the faithful Abraham.

He passes to another comforting passage, this

time from Habakkuk: "The righteous man shall live by faith." But Paul comes to it in this Epistle through the jarring curses of the law, and the redemption which the crucifixion worked — straining, as it may seem to us, the connexion if not the meaning of the passages. Had he meant that no one could be justified by the works of the law, and yet whoever failed in them had been accursed; but now Christ, hanging upon the tree, had abolished the curse for his believers, and made firm their justification through faith?

He next argues that Christ is *the* seed, in whom the covenant with Abraham is confirmed. The law was added because of transgressions, till the seed should come, to whom the promise had been made, this promise which enures to the salvation of those who believe in Christ. Till then, we were wards of the law, but now are no longer in its tutelage. At this point, Paul's great conclusion — and his own spirit — flings itself free: "For ye are all sons of God, through faith in Christ Jesus." And the conclusion is immediately substantiated: "For as many of you as were baptised into Christ did put on Christ. There can be neither Jew nor Greek, there can be neither bond nor free, there can be no male and female: for ye are all one man in Christ Jesus." Yet still the clinging Jew in Paul turns back again to reassure his converts, as he once had needed to reassure himself: "And if ye are Christ's,

Q

then are ye Abraham's seed, heirs according to
promise." But while in tutelage as children, until
the time appointed by the Father, we were in bondage to the rudiments, the A-B-C's, perhaps, the
elemental spirits (στοῖχεια τοῦ κόσμου; where did
Paul get this word so much used in primary education and in philosophy ?), until in the fulness of
time God sent his Son, born under the law, that he
might redeem those under the law, and we might
receive the adoption of sons : would ye who now
know God turn back to the beggarly elements !

Thus he fiercely clinches his argument; as in
times past he often may have driven it home to
himself. One must remember that none of Paul's
extant Epistles was written till many years after
the vision on the road ; their fully reasoned out
assurances may have come to their author slowly
through toil and struggle.[1] And how fierce and living are the arguments in these Epistles ! arguments
which Paul must so often have levelled at his own
difficulties. Indeed, did he ever altogether cast off
his reliance on these arguments which had established
his freedom from the law ? In this Epistle to the
Galatians, at least, he is not yet satisfied that he has
convinced them fully, for he allegorises from the

[1] Though it is hazardous to rely on Acts for the exact speeches
of Paul, Acts xiii. 16–41 seems to give an early stage of Paul's
preaching before he had fully worked out the arguments of his
Epistles.

two sons of Abraham, the one by a handmaid, born
after the flesh, the other by the free woman, born
through promise, — the promise which is unto us.
Then he warns them not to receive circumcision;
for in Christ neither circumcision nor uncircumcision availeth, *but faith working through love.*

In these last words, Paul's argument, and he with
it, again flings off its fetters; and he continues,
admonishing the Galatians practically with the
beautiful disencumbered ethics of Christ. Closing,
again he warns them against those who insist on
circumcision, and do not themselves keep the law
(no more than Cephas did !). They would glory in
your flesh ! "But far be it from me to glory, save
in the cross of our Lord Jesus Christ, through which
the world has been crucified to me, and I unto the
world. For neither is circumcision anything, nor
uncircumcision, *but a new creature.* And as many
as shall walk by this rule, peace be upon them, and
mercy, and upon the Israel of God. From henceforth let no man trouble me : for I bear branded on
my body the marks of Jesus. The grace of our
Lord Jesus Christ be with your spirit. Amen."

Paul's phrases have long since become pious
commonplaces, emptied or filled with meaning
to suit the user. But Paul, when he said that
through the cross of Christ the world had been
crucified to him and he to the world, meant verily
that his old life — his sinful nature — had gone

out of him, and was replaced with the eternal life of Christ, and that thereby he was literally a new creature, from which the old had passed away. We must accustom ourselves to read in such words of Paul the veritable, almost corporeal, meaning which they carried for him, if we would form an idea of the adjustment which it was given him to attain.

That may now be approached through a sheer and well-nigh literal acceptance of what he is saying in the opening chapters of the first Epistle to the Corinthians. He is beseeching them to have done with divisions, one saying, "I am of Paul," and another, "I am of Apollos"; and he is glad that he himself baptised so few of them, lest they might say they were baptised in his name. And thereupon, according to the greatness of his nature, Paul lifts the matter above their small contentions, into the region of the truth of Christ. "For Christ sent me not to baptise, but to preach the Gospel: not in wisdom of words, lest the cross of Christ should be made void. For the word of the cross is to them that are perishing foolishness; but unto us which are being saved it is the power of God" — δύναμις θεοῦ — literally, or rather, verily, the power of God. . . . "We preach Christ crucified," a stumbling for the Jews and foolishness to the Gentiles, "but unto them that are called, both Jews and Greeks, Christ the power of God, and the wisdom of God"

— again, literally and veritably. And then when
Paul has referred to his own feebleness, and theirs,
he tells them he has not preached persuasive words
of wisdom, but set forth a *demonstration* of *spirit*
and *power:* "that your faith should not stand in
the wisdom of men, but in the power of God,"
literally again, ἐν δυνάμει θεοῦ. "For the Kingdom
of God is not in word but in power."

He shows them that as the spirit of man understands human things, so "none knoweth the things
of God save the spirit of God," which "we received"
— again, literally. "Now the natural man receiveth
not the things of the spirit of God; for they are
foolishness unto him . . . but we have the mind of
Christ," — we have been given the mind of Christ,
and it is that which within us, in the place of our
old minds, understands the things of God. "Know
ye not that ye are a temple of God, and the spirit of
God dwelleth in you?" He speaks figuratively,
but also with absolute literalness: "the spirit of
God dwelleth in you." Then, showing them how
that he is, before the world, a fool for Christ's
sake, naked, buffeted, and blessing when reviled, he
admonishes them as to their sinfulness with that
splendid religious ethics of his, and brings his exhortation back to this same clinching question, which
was to be taken literally: "Know ye not that your
body is a temple of the Holy Spirit which is in you,
which you have from God?"

We are moving in the atmosphere of Paul's adjustment, and may now in some degree appreciate its contents and periphery. His large nature needed an assurance manifold and comprehensive, satisfying to his heart as well as mind, and including the salvation of his beloved fellows. As a foundation, his feet were planted in the monotheism of the prophets of his race: "We know that no idol is anything in the world, and that there is no god but one . . . to us there is one God, the Father, of whom are all things, and we unto him, and one Lord Jesus Christ, through whom are all things, and we through him."[1]

Paul realises Christ as "the image of the invisible God, the first-born of all creation; . . . all things have been created through him and unto him; and he is before all things, and in him all things consist . . . in him dwelleth all the fulness of the Godhead bodily" (Col. i. 15; ii. 9). "In whom we have redemption, the forgiveness of sins. . . . For it was the good pleasure of the Father . . . through him to reconcile all things unto himself, having made peace through the blood of his cross" (Col. i). We "believe in him who raised Jesus our Lord from the dead, who was delivered up for our trespasses, and was raised for our justification. Being therefore justified by faith, we have peace with God through our Lord Jesus Christ" (Rom. iv. 25; v. 1).

[1] 1 Cor. viii. 4. Cf. Acts xxiv. 14; xxxvi. 6.

Paul's conception of the nature and function of
Christ is one of the wonderful things of history.
With him, God, the Father of all, is the source of
power and life and love. But the fulness of the
Godhead dwelleth bodily in Christ, and it is in Christ
that Paul virtually lives and moves and has his being: unto the measure of whose fulness tendeth the
stature of the full-grown man; he is the absolute
standard; his love constraineth us, and the spirit of
Christ is life within us — that which does away
with the sinfulness and mortality of the flesh.
"The free gift of God is eternal life in Christ Jesus
our Lord" (Rom. vi. 23).   "But ye are not in the
flesh, but in the spirit, if so be that the spirit of God
dwelleth in you.   But if any man hath not (literally
"hath not") the spirit of Christ, he is none of his.
And if Christ is in you, the body is dead because of
sin; but the spirit is life because of righteousness.
But if the spirit of him that raised up Jesus from
the dead dwelleth in you, he that raised up Christ
Jesus from the dead shall quicken also your mortal
bodies through his spirit that dwelleth in you"
(Rom. viii. 9).

It is hazardous to attempt to state Paul's thoughts,
his convictions, his expressions of the power through
which he lived, in any language save his own;
and even then we may doubt whether we grasp his
words in the significance they bore for him.   Justification by faith! surely: yet how that legally ar-

rived at principle pales before the living Christ in whom is life! As Paul had risen from the law, and had wrestled himself free from the bondage of its arguments, his adjustment was to be no longer of the reason only, or even mainly. It was of the whole man, comforted, assured, dwelling in the lordship and power of the loving and saving Christ.

"Though our outward man is decaying, yet our inward man is renewed day by day. For our light affliction, which is for the moment, worketh for us more and more an eternal weight of glory . . . we know that if the earthly house of our tabernacle be dissolved, we have a building from God, a house not made with hands, eternal, in the heavens. . . . For the love of Christ constraineth us, since we judge that as one died for all, therefore all died; and he died for all, that they which live should no longer live unto themselves, but unto him who for their sakes died and rose again. Wherefore we henceforth know no man after the flesh; even though we have known Christ after the flesh, yet now we know him so no more. Wherefore if any man is in Christ, he is a new creature: the old things have passed away; behold, they are become new. But all things are from God, who reconciled us to himself through Christ. . . . God was in Christ reconciling the world unto himself" (2 Cor. iv and v).

And how had not the great Apostle, to whom the word of reconciliation had been committed (2 Cor.

v. 19), to whom had been vouchsafed visions, up-
liftings to the heavens, and the revelation of Christ
within himself, how had he not felt the power of God
in his own weakness, when he had prayed that the
"stake in the flesh" might be removed, and the
answer had been : "My grace is sufficient for thee;
for power is perfected in weakness."

One need not pause to say that in Paul's adjustment, justification by faith — the spirit of Christ in
the believer ! — is organically united with all righteousness, and separated from all sin and sinfulness,
an ethical union and separation which is expanded
and emphasised throughout Paul's Epistles. The
final bond of all, and even the inmost principle of
salvation, is love — the love of God, the love of
Christ, the love of man. "Who shall separate us from
the love of Christ ? shall tribulation, or anguish, or
persecution, or famine, or nakedness, or peril, or
sword ? Nay, in all these things we are more than
conquerors through him that loved us. For I am
persuaded, that neither death, nor life, nor angels,
nor principalities, nor things present nor things to
come, nor powers, nor height, nor depth, nor any
other creature, shall be able to separate us from the
love of God, which is in Christ Jesus our Lord."

All spiritual gifts, all manifestations of the power
of life within us, are they not of the same spirit
of God ? diversities of workings, and the same God
who worketh all things in all ? And are we not all

members of the same body of Christ ? For the obtaining of these gifts of the Spirit, these freely bestowed powers of God, which are one in their source of Christ, "a still more excellent way show I unto you." And Paul breaks into his lyric chapter on the indispensable and excellent sufficiency of love, in that adjustment which unites the relationships between men with the relationship of man to God. It is this necessary principle and fact of love, this having within himself the mind of Christ, which will not permit Paul to rest in any adjustment, or assurance of salvation, that does not include the salvation of his loved fellow-beings: "Wherefore, my brethren beloved and longed for, my joy and my crown, so stand fast in the Lord, my beloved" (Phil. iv. 1). "I say the truth in Christ, I lie not, my conscience bearing witness with me in the Holy Spirit, that I have great sorrow and unceasing pain in my heart. For I could wish that I myself were anathema from Christ for my brethren's sake, my kinsmen after the flesh, who are Israelites" (Rom. ix. 1).

These are the horns, not so much of Paul's dilemma as of his full adjustment and salvation. The fervour of his Epistles, which may become a veritable *furor*, belongs to his passion to save men in Christ. It pours through the Epistles to the Philippians and the Thessalonians — through all his Epistles indeed : " For I am jealous over you with a godly

jealousy! . . . Of the Jews five times received I
forty stripes save one. Thrice was I beaten with
rods, once was I stoned, thrice I suffered shipwreck
. . . in journeyings often, in perils in the city, in
perils in the wilderness . . . in labour and travail,
in hunger and thirst, in cold and nakedness. Beside
those things that are without, there is that which
presseth upon me daily, anxiety for all the churches.
Who is weak, and I am not weak? who is made to
stumble, and I burn not?" (2 Cor. xi. 2 *sqq*.).
"For what is our hope, or joy, or crown of glorying?
Are not even ye, before our Lord Jesus at his coming?
. . . for now we live if ye stand fast in the Lord"
(1 Thess. ii. 19; iii. 8).

In common with the disciples of Jesus, Paul
shared the expectation of the near coming of the
Lord, — even before their generation should have
passed away. Questions were rife in the first Christian communities as to the manner of the resurrection, and even as to the relative advantages or prec-
edence, on that day, of the living and the dead.
"But we would not have you ignorant, brethren,
concerning them that fall asleep. . . . For if we
believe that Jesus died and rose again, even so them
also that are fallen asleep in Jesus will God bring
with him. For this we say unto you by the word
of the Lord, that we that are alive, that are left until
the coming of the Lord, shall in no wise precede
them that are fallen asleep. For the Lord himself

shall descend from heaven with a shout, with the voice of the archangel, and with the trump of God: and the dead in Christ shall rise first: then we that are alive, that are left, shall together with them be caught up in the clouds, to meet the Lord in the air: and so shall we ever be with the Lord" (1 Thess. iv. 13–17). Without a realisation of this conviction of Paul's one cannot understand all parts of the fifteenth chapter of First Corinthians, as when he says: "We shall not all sleep, but we shall all be changed, in a moment, in the twinkling of an eye, at the last trump: for the trumpet shall sound, and the dead shall be raised incorruptible, and we shall be changed. For this corruption must put on incorruption, and this mortal must put on immortality."

Mightily Paul preached the resurrection, without which his own peace, his adjustment, his assurance of salvation, were an idle song, as he knew. "If in this life only we have hoped in Christ, we are of all men most pitiable. . . . If the dead are not raised, let us eat and drink, for to-morrow we die."

And his comfort of assurance lay in the life in Christ, and the sure expectation of the coming of the Lord. Wherefore, in the midst of stripes and persecutions, his heart did steadily rejoice, and bade his brethren also to rejoice: "Rejoice in the Lord always: again I will say, rejoice. . . . The Lord is at hand. In nothing be anxious. . . . And the peace of God, which passeth all understanding, shall guard your hearts and your thoughts in Christ Jesus. Finally, brethren, whatsoever things are true, whatsoever things are honorable, whatsoever things are just, whatsoever things are pure, whatsoever things are lovely, whatsoever things are of good report; if there be any virtue, and if there be any praise, think on these things" (Phil. iv).

Thus Paul joins together the factors of his peace, which rested in the Lord, in his near coming, in the joy of his own and his fellows' salvation, — saved in part through his ministry; which rested also in purity of life, and in the love which worketh all things in love; love which is very near to knowledge, very near to the realisation of the purposes of God. "For this cause I bow my knees unto the Father, from whom every family in heaven and on earth is named, that he would grant you, according to the riches of his glory, that ye may be strengthened with power through his spirit in the inward man; that Christ may dwell in your hearts through faith; to the end that ye, being rooted and grounded in love, may be strong to apprehend with all the saints what is the breadth and length and height and depth, and to know the love of Christ which passeth knowledge, that ye may be filled unto all the fulness of God" (Eph. iii. 14–19).

This last sentence, whether Paul wrote it, or it be by another hand, is Paul, in the richness and power of his manifold nature and his acceptance of Christ.

CHAPTER XI

AUGUSTINE

IN the three centuries elapsing between the death of Paul and the birth of Augustine, Christianity had pressed itself with vital insistency upon the Greco-Roman world, until it had won recognition as the religion of the Empire. If the Gospel had triumphed, it was also to some extent led captive through its adaptation to the ways in which the centuries of its reception could understand and accept it. Yet, at the same time, the Gospel, or whatever constituted the vitality of Christianity, was constantly advancing through emergence and disclaimer, keeping itself free from those elements of its environment which it could not accept or assimilate without impairing its organic consistency and power.

These are the two general and intimately complementary phases of the process resulting in the Christianity of the fourth century. Both are represented in Augustine. But his life evolved elements of its own, those personal features of his own spiritual growth which completed the Latin understanding of Christianity, or, if one will, the mode of its reception by the Latin world. Latin Christianity becomes itself in Augustine, who represents, *resumes* in his experience and efforts the processes through which it had become what it was, not in the year 354 when he was born, but in the year 430, when he died, having finished his work. For the matter of its growth, the contents of its mutations, since apostolic times, were purified and finished in his person. The greater, or at least the better, part of what was to endure of prior teaching was taken up and transmitted through the unifying and somewhat transforming personality of Augustine. He forms the basis, and even the structure, of the Western Christianity of the next thousand years.

Regarded from another point of view, Augustine exemplifies the tremendous power carried in the main interest or most vital energy of an age. What would he have been, what would his life have amounted to, had he not accepted Christianity? In it he developed his powers, and brought his faculties to actualisation. He was bred to a profession which had lost all creativeness, and stood for the final sterility of Greco-Roman culture. As long as he remained a professor of rhetoric, — of pagan literature and oratory, — he moved in that dry atmosphere, his own faculties unvitalised, literally *unformed*, for lack of a certain purpose and a goal. Then he was led to become a Christian. With his conversion, gradually, by no means at once, he and all his faculties and all his knowledge gained form,

and a unity of inspiration, till they filled and expanded with the fulness and the power of Christ.

The vast majority of the people of any age are
busied with their narrow daily interests. Their
further hopes and fears are not insistent; they are
but slightly moved either by religious devotion or
spiritual unrest. It is but the remnant that experiences religious fervour or anxiety. The rest
accept suggestions, go with the tendency set by this
remnant, and so pass from one spiritual dulness to
another. Making these provisos, one may speak of
the pagan world, in the first centuries of the Christian
era, as restless and touched with yearning for a divine
salvation. The words of Augustine which have
always been taken as the key-note of the movements
of his soul, were applicable to that pagan world:
"fecisti nos ad te, et inquietum est cor nostrum
donec requiescat in te." Manifestly, the pagan
world was seeking a new spiritual deliverance.

The Christian Gospel was a means to this salvation, a balm for this unrest. In it, to note its tangible form and the manner of its presentation,
Christ was the Saviour, and the healer of bodies as
well as souls. He offered eternal life, in the place of
mortality and death. He cured sin as a disease,
he the good physician, his ministers also healing in
the power of the Spirit. He saved, moreover,
from the demons which possessed and terrified the
world, causing insanity, disease, and sin. His

apostles, his bishops and preachers, were likewise casters out of demons, bringers of sanity, *exorcisers:* they were expelling sin and demons from among men. In accordance with these functions of its ministers, the Gospel moved in the power of love and charity. Those accepting it formed a community, devoted to its transmission and to the care of the human means and instruments. Each community provided for its teachers, for its widows and orphans; for the sick, for slaves, for prisoners in the mines, and for the bodies of the dead. The Church, moreover, that is, the universal and duly constituted body of believers acting through their ordained representatives, was rapidly becoming the fountain-head of divine power on earth. For the Church possessed the authority to interpret and declare the contents of the faith and the meaning of the Old Testament, with its proofs of Christ and wealth of prototypal institutions; also the authority not only to interpret, but even to make, the New Testament, by establishing its canon; and finally the authority to order and administer the Christian rites of baptism and the Lord's Supper, which were becoming sacramental mysteries, and to which other sacraments were soon added. The sacramental ritual grew apace, developing what was Christian in origin and adopting unconsciously much from the world to which believers, before conversion, had belonged. Naturally these did not altogether lay

R

aside their former intellectual and spiritual habits
on becoming Christians. Dwelling in an atmosphere of religious emotion, the uncritical souls of
these early Christians were fertile receptacles for
superstitions which, wearing new masks or old, were
the same in Christianity and paganism.

Yet, although founded on concrete revelation,
and representing transmitted authority, and feeding
upon superstitions, the Church, which was the body
of believers, and in a mystic sense the body of Christ,
also admitted reason and reasonableness, as a co-
ordinate determinant of its rejections and accept-
ances. The Gospel was a faith with all; with some
it might also be a philosophy. So, just as the
Church accepted superstitions and elements of
sacramental magic from the pagan world, it also
appropriated its knowledge and its reason; and
soon maintained, in self-justification, that pagan
philosophy, so far as it contained elements of truth,
received them from the Christian God, or borrowed
them from the Scriptures. The believing communities constituting the Church of Christ made
a people newly set apart to God; yet they conceived
themselves to have existed from the beginning
as the chosen Israel of God, the human vessel of
divine truth. Though still unrecognised by the
Jews and the pagan multitude, the Church had
become with Origen, in the third century, the all-
embracing and all-ordering kingdom, the κόσμος τοῦ

κόσμου.[1] With Augustine, in greater power, it is,
had always been, shall always be, the City of God.

If a new religion, flung into the world, is to endure,
it must remain itself, and not become something
else. Yet if it would be accepted by the world,
it must present itself in intelligible modes, receive
from the world whatever is pertinent and not
hostile to its spirit, and adapt itself to the world
in matters of the world — thus rendering unto
Cæsar what is Cæsar's. While it cannot be eclectic,
it may be selective and synthetic.

This dual need of self-preservation and adaptation
to the world pressed upon the new-born Christian
faith. In meeting it the Gospel's energies took form
in three phases of constructive action : the organisation of the Christian Church, the ordering of the
Christian life, the formulation of the Christian
faith. They are not to be too sharply distinguished
in treatment, seeing how dynamically interwoven
in their action were these phases of Christian energy.
A vast amount of learning has been devoted to their
elucidation.

An outer, as it were, secular organisation of the
Church was needed for the preservation and regulation of the life and faith of the Christian communities, and even for the maintenance of life and order,
in those centuries of political disintegration. The

[1] *Contra Celsum*, viii, Chapters 67–75, cited by Harnack in
The Mission and Extension of Christianity, etc.

Latin, or Roman, Catholic Church (our mind is fixed upon the West), which gradually took form in response to this need, may not improperly be viewed as the final creation of the Roman political genius, though its creation was inspired with other motives than those which had made great the Republic and the Empire. The Church was the embodiment of Christian unity and Christian order, of Christ's divine authority on earth, of fellowship with Christ and participation in salvation. The authority which Christ was recorded to have delivered to the Apostles, became in the course of time vested in the bishops as their successors. These were ranged under their metropolitans, and eventually under the bishop of Rome; they acted corporately in councils. The Church was intrusted with the ministration of the Sacraments, which were the means of grace, the vehicles of life, without which no one could be saved. There was, therefore, no salvation without the Church: Salus extra ecclesiam non est, says Cyprian. Upon this conviction, and its own grand organisation, the Church was to hold itself erect while the Empire crumbled about it.

Obviously the organising of the Church and its investment with authority over many things of this world, according to the needs of an earthly society, could not but result in its partial secularisation. The springs of the spirit, inconveniently vagrant in Apostolic times, were gathered to ecclesiastic channels, and administered through sacerdotal conduits, through which alone, and also unfailingly, flowed the divine grace. In conflict with the revolt of Montanist enthusiasts, in the late second century, the Church maintained its exclusive official authority over the gifts of the Spirit; maintained, as well, its authority to promulgate Christian doctrine and order Christian life.

The need of an authoritative organ to declare, and keep declaring, what was and what was not Christian doctrine, had promoted the organisation of the authoritative Church. The rapid encroachments of a semi-Christian Gnosticism in the second century threatened the Gospel's existence as a definite fact and revelation. In order to combat Gnosticism, throw it off, and keep Christianity from becoming a congeries of phantasies, the Church proclaimed the Apostolic Creed and fixed the Apostolic Canon of the New Testament. Next, a reciprocally correlated conception was reached (by Irenæus) of the Gospel both as the revealed rule of belief and conduct, and as the way of veritable transformation of corrupt and mortal manhood through the spirit of Christ. Under the former aspect, eternal life would appear as a reward; under the latter, it was a supernatural gift. From these broad bases the formulation of dogma proceeded according to the twofold need of presenting

the Gospel in conformity to the intellectual in-
sistencies of the Greco-Roman world, and of con-
demning what was not the Gospel and could not
make part of Christian truth. Accordingly the
doctrine of the nature of Christ, and of the two
natures of Christ, divine and human, was worked
out with infinite toil and fierce anathemas. In this
central field of Christian dogma, the Church argued
in the categories of Greek (mainly Neoplatonic)
philosophy; although, in the Latin West, theologians
also employed the terminology and conceptions of
the Roman Law. While the formulation of these
dogmas proceeded largely through the disavowal
of propositions held erroneous, it was also a creative
process, resulting in the establishment of positive
propositions. They are contained in the Nicene
Creed. That did not contravene the teaching
either of Christ or the Apostles, and held to the
realities of the Christian Gospel. It was a necessary
formulation of the Gospel, if all manner of pagan
concepts were to be excluded. Yet it was not
the Gospel, but a restatement of it in terms of
Greek philosophy. If the Creed contradicted many
a thesis of Greek philosophy, Greek philosophy had
nevertheless entered its structure. As touching
these dogmas, the Latin West followed the Hellenic
East; but of itself turned to a more intimate wrestling with the problem of sin, and the relations
between the human will and divine grace; in which

struggle he who proved himself the orthodox protagonist was Augustine.

The Church; dogma; the Christian life. The last
was builded from the matter of its own living appro-
priation of the Faith, and yet was affected by the
need to accept or reject the pagan life about it. It
began in those inspired enthusiasms of the new
Faith, when the recipients of the Spirit spoke with
tongues, or prophesied, or taught, or healed with
laying on of hands. If there were dissensions,
charity also overflowed. The widow, the fatherless,
the poor, the sick, were cared for. Abundant
giving, extending even to the abandonment of lands
and all possessions, marked the lives of the believers,
and from the first called for official administration.
As Christianity spread among the Gentiles, the
converts naturally withdrew from pagan worship
and from festivals or ceremonies involving sacrifices
or recognition of the pagan gods; withdrew also
from the games of the circus and gladiatorial com-
bats, which shocked the newly awakened Christian
conscience. But many complicated problems rose
for believers: what trades might they pursue, or
follow what professions, when pagan practices
and observances touched the whole round of daily
life ? Could Christians serve in the army, when
the military oath involved recognition of the Emperor's divinity ? These exigencies might be met
according to circumstances and individual conviction.

Profounder dilemmas were involved in the question of the pagan literature and pagan philosophy. Might Christians teach, or even study, that profane literature ? This was never answered on principle, but was solved through acquiescence in the need of education, which could be had only through pagan books. As to pagan philosophy, there were sharp divergences. Some would have none of it, or at least so proclaimed; but it was as necessary as the breath of life, necessary indeed for those doctors who would state the Faith in terms satisfying to their own philosophically educated minds, or in a manner to be convincing to educated pagans. Neither was this problem solved on principle, but was worked out, as Jerome and Augustine worked it out through the needs of their lives and labours.

An even more ideal question — beauty. High-minded Christians sought to turn from the lures of sculptured ivory and living flesh to the beauties of the Christian spirit — the beauty of the soul and God. Plato had felt and thought the like before them. Connected with beauty were lust and love, which offered the most insistent of all problems. Augustine was to reach a solution filling the utmost reaches of his soul, as he merged or proportioned human loves in the love of God. But, before him, the Christian communities had gone far toward setting the virgin state above the married, and toward demanding celibacy of bishops and presbyters; while the most prodigious solution of this problem, the Christian working answer to the plea for severance from the lusts of paganism and the sinful world, had been given in the hermit lives of hundreds of imitators of St. Anthony, and in the even mightier commencements of corporate monasticism.

Did the hot sun of western Northern Africa breed fiery, sensual, and spiritually grasping temperaments ? It was an eager, even violent land. The people who were not Christians held ardently to their religions, hating the Christians who stood aloof from long-cherished practices. Nowhere else was persecution so fiercely called for by the pagan population. On their side, the Christians were fervent. The martyrs passed to the arena with devoted constancy. Montanism had come originally from Phrygia; but that unmanageable, irreconcilable form of Christianity flourished nowhere as in Africa. There it denounced the worldliness, and scorned the authority, of the Church, itself spurning all adaptation to the world. And there Tertullian, greatest of Christian advocates and of Latin theologians before Augustine, became a Montanist through his headstrong ardour and tenacious egotism.

Augustine was African by birth and breeding. He was a man of passion and desire, of restless temper, gifted with an analytic and constructive mind, and destined, under the impulsion of Christianity, to prove a spiritual genius. He was loving and devoted, and yet a constraining egotism marshalled his faculties, impelled and informed their action, and drove him on to the giving of himself to God or rather to the winning of God. From his youth he had thought on his ultimate adjustment with life; and he became ever more interested, if not absorbed, in reaching some assurance, even an assurance of salvation. No small subjective satisfaction could accord with his largeness of mind. Assurance of his personal salvation must include the final settlement of his opinions, convictions as they became, regarding everything of salient import for human destiny. It was a necessity of his nature to bring his thoughts on God and man and all things into a religious unison, wherein they should work together for the assurance of the soul's salvation. If in his *Soliloquies*, near the time of his conversion, he desired to know only God and the soul, it was because his previous thoughts had resolved everything of vital interest for man into the relationship between the soul and God.

Primarily and always, Augustine sought his peace — in God. But as he reached the first stage of certitude in his conversion, his energies expanded, and took form in labours to complete his own salvation, and, through a vindication of true doctrine, safeguard the faith of the Church. Henceforth

the arguments with which he maintained Christian
truth and the Church's authority against Manichæans, against pagans, against Donatists and
Pelagians, served likewise to substantiate and perfect
the peace which he had won. For that peace
could be secured only through a spiritual progress
which should include the overthrow of every threaten-
ing argument, and the settlement of the problems
pressing on the soul.

There is universal significance in the course taken
by Augustine's adjustment, in the manner, if one
will, of his working himself out of previous insufficient
adjustments till he found refuge in the Christian
God, — a refuge which he was to make large enough
for all. For the universality of his desiring and investigating nature led him on through all the stages
by which, before the time of his conversion, the
Church had won its triumph over the passion and
the reason of the heathen world, and also had
kept itself the true Church of Christ. But Augustine's adjustment will lead further still. For,
living when many a searching Christian question
was unsettled, through one and the same series of
intellectual, or, rather, spiritual, achievements,
he perfected his deliverance and completed Christian
doctrine.

A general knowledge of Augustine's life may be
assumed. Recently a charming book has been
made of it: *Saint Augustin*, by Louis Bertrand.

One may say that he did not cease to be pagan in his mode of life until he had become Christian in his convictions. Only thus was he freed from lusts of the flesh, and from a manner of living ministering to them in a moderate degree. It is to our purpose to follow the mental steps leading him from one and another opinion not in accord with Christianity. For each of these opinions represented an obstacle to the acceptance of Christianity, and at the same time a section of the path leading to it.

Certain elementary Christian lessons of his childhood were never quite forgotten. They seem to have left a wavering longing or affection in his mind for the wonderful figure of the Saviour; the name of Jesus was always sweet to him. And yet it was but as a fugitive sound to hark back to, — as with a hound that is worried, having lost the scent. His school education at first had no religious bearing; but gradually became pagan in its influence, as he progressed in grammar and rhetoric and the study of the profane literature which made the medium of these disciplines. Evidently his reading of Cicero's *Hortensius*, with its alluring persuasions toward philosophy, made a deep impression, to judge from his frequent mention of it. His reading it may have been an awakening. In after life, he said it turned his prayers toward God, and filled him with longing for wisdom, which is with God. The book pleased him especially since it held no brief for any sect, but rather enkindled within him the loving quest of wisdom. It lacked one thing which had touched his heart, the name of Christ. And still the Scriptures themselves, because of their humble guise, repelled the young rhetorician (*Conf.* iii, 4 and 5).

He heard that name indeed in the vain mouthings of the Manichæans, as he said afterwards; and partly with that lure they drew him to their sect. Probably the impression of the evil and the suffering in the world, and his lack of philosophic enlightenment, made his mind a guest-chamber for their opinions; which were full of fantastic fables, and heavy with material views of God. At the same time he was painfully stumbling over the Old Testament narratives, of patriarchs with many wives, and commended by the mouth of God, although their conduct was such as men no longer could approve; for he did not then comprehend the righteousness which always is the same, and yet may ordain what is suitable only for a certain time (*Conf.* iii, 7); nor had he learned, as afterwards from Ambrose, to interpret the Old Testament "spiritaliter" in its allegorical truth. If he only could have "conceived spiritual substance," he would quickly have thrown out the Manichæan arguments (*Conf.* v, 14).

So in those years of his early manhood at Carthage he kept company with the Manichæans, and also dallied with the *Mathematici* (astrologers), thinking well of them because they neither sacrificed nor

prayed to any spirit to direct their divinations. He
did not realise the folly of their doctrine that a man's
sin or sinlessness is fixed by the stars. A certain
wise physician pointed out to him the deceit, or at
most haphazard agreement, of their vain prognostica-
tions, — and yet he clung to them, for want of a sure
refutation.

It was also in these Carthaginian years that the
death of a friend showed him the futility of "spilling
his soul upon the sand in loving that which was
mortal as if it were not," — a first lesson in the discipline which directs the mind toward the love of God
and the love of men in God. Although he deemed
beauty to be the chief element of the lovable, the
lower forms of beauty held his thoughts. Num
amamus aliquid nisi pulchrum, exclaimed his
sensuous or æsthetic nature; while his questing
spirit asked what is beauty? what is this which
draws us to the things we love? He made his first
essay on authorship, with a book upon this subject,
entitled "de pulchro et apto," "The beautiful and
fit." In later life he looked back upon this book
through the altered perspective of maturer thoughts:
"But I saw not yet the essential matter in thy art,
Almighty One, who alone makest marvellous things;
and my mind was going through corporeal forms;
and I was defining and distinguishing what was
beautiful in itself, what was fit, and what gains grace
through adaptation to something; and I was

furnishing my argument with corporeal illustrations.
Also I turned me to the nature of the soul, and the
false view I had of spiritual substances did not permit me to perceive the truth. . . . I was averting
my mind from the incorporeal thing toward linea-
ments and colors and swelling magnitudes, and
because I could not find them in the soul, I thought
I could not see my soul. And since in virtue I
loved peace, and in vice hated discord, I saw unity
in the one and division in the other; and the rational mind as well as the essence of truth and of
the *summum bonum* seemed set in that unity, while
in that division I deemed there dwelt I know not
what substance of irrational life, an essential *summum malum* — not only substance but life, and yet
not dependent on thee, my God, from whom are
all things" (*Conf.* iv, 15).

Some years before, he had been given the *Categories* of Aristotle, which he first gaped at as something divine, then quickly mastered, but only to
find little help; since he could not imagine that the
attributes of God were in God as in a subject, seeing
that God is each of his attributes — as his magnitude,
his beauty. Perhaps Augustine's dissatisfaction
with the little Aristotelian masterpiece was a stage
in his approach to more spiritual thoughts of God;
but not till long afterwards did he learn to know
that beauty, which God was, from which the creature
beauties had so long kept him.

The approach of his thirtieth year found him still in Carthage, but very restless. Why not try his fortune as a professor of rhetoric in Rome ? He set sail, with letters from the Manichæans of Carthage, although he no longer approved their doctrines. In Rome he realised that he and they must soon part company; though he still had not freed himself from the thought of God as material substance, nor from conceiving evil as a substance gross as earth or thin as air, yet always some sort of bulk or body, which the good God could not have created. He still thought that God was limited and finite in relation to evil. He imagined the Saviour as issuing (porrectum) from a mass of the brightest divine substance; — how could he have been born of the Virgin and not have suffered defilement as part of her flesh ?

Amidst these doubts, his mind turned naturally to the chief advocates of philosophic doubt, the Academics — Carneades and others belonging to the later Academy called of Plato. They seemed the wisest in holding all things to be in doubt, because of man's inability to know the truth.

In this state of mind, looking for adjustment and assurance, and yet not unhappy in the play of philosophic doubt, Augustine accepted a call to fill the city chair of Rhetoric in Milan; it was in the year 384, and he was still but thirty years of age. Milan was the usual residence of the imperial court, then Catholic. The town was Christian, with sympathies torn between Catholics and Arians; and there Ambrose was bishop. On his arrival, Augustine openly shook off Manichæan affiliations, and resumed the position of a Christian catechumen; for as such his mother had inscribed him when a child. He lost no time in paying his respects to Ambrose, his admiration for whom was soon to deepen into reverence.

This is the period of Augustine's "Conversion," touching which there is the later devotional testimony of his *Confessions*. But earlier works, written at the time, indicate a different mood, and disclose the philosophic questions then busying his mind. The *Confessions* are not *Wahrheit und Dichtung;* but they are Wahrheit and piety. Ten years of thought and study, of living and feeling, had elapsed since he left Milan a baptised Christian. During those years, his convictions had grown surer and more definite, had become vibrant with emotion, and Augustine had acquired the habit of devout expression. The devoutness of those *Confessions*, and *their* power of feeling, scarcely made part of his nature in the more inchoate period of his faith. Yet they do not contradict, so much as supplement, the earlier writings, which by reason of their tentative as well as academic character scantily expressed the emotional crises of that time.

The character of Ambrose drew Augustine toward

s

the Catholic fold. He listened to his preaching diligently. He learned from it the method of spiritual, that is to say, allegorical interpretation of the Old Testament — its hard places, which "when I had taken them literally, I was killed — occidebar." *Littera occidit*, the letter killeth — that he now learned, and was to understand in time how the spirit maketh to live. This method of interpretation cleared his mind of any lingering regard for the arguments which the Manichæans brought against the Church. But he inclined the more strongly toward certain of the Greek philosophers, and yet "could not commit the cure of his soul's languor to them, because they were without the healing name of Christ." This languor of the half dilettante pagan soul was, in fact, vigorously expelled by the energy of the Christian faith, when that had entered Augustine.

The months passed, Augustine filling the duties of his professorship; studying also and constantly turning over in his mind, or discussing with friends from Africa, the opinions of the different philosophers. He was still held by the comforts and pleasures of the flesh, and but for his belief in a life after death, would even have awarded the palm of the ethical discussion to Epicurus (*Conf.* vi, 16). He had put from him anthropomorphic conceptions of God, and yet could not conceive him as incorporeal; but rather as something corporeal infused in the world and diffused boundlessly about it, always incorruptible and unchangeable: "So that the earth should have Thee, and the heaven have Thee, and all things be bounded in Thee, and Thou nowhere bounded" (*Conf.* vii, 1). Still the problem of evil plagued him — as he set himself to understand how that man's free will (liberum voluntatis arbitrium) was the cause of our evil-doing and God's just judgement. But how then? did not the good God make him, and that will of his which preferred evil? then why should he be punished? And he began to imagine the creation vast and manifold, and yet finite, with God surrounding and penetrating it, everywhere infinite — as an infinite sea holding and everywhere penetrating a huge though finite sponge. Where, then, in such a universe made by omnipotent goodness, could there be evil? He was sore perplexed.

Yet, at least he was able to throw off all credence in the horoscopes cast by the *mathematici*, astrologers. (Thus had such godless superstitions clung to him!) For he considered seriously how different were the fortunes even of twins, and others born at the same instant. And still he could find no outcome to the problem, whence is evil? God alone, and no man, knew how he was afflicted with it!

He was to gain light from the works of the Greek Neoplatonists, translated (for Augustine could read but little Greek) by a rhetorician and philoso-

pher named C. Marius Victorinus, who in the end
had himself become a Christian (cf. *Conf.* viii, 2).
It seemed to him afterwards that the hand of God
had given him these books. He learned from them,
although in different words, and set forth with many
reasons, that "in the beginning was the Word and
the Word was with God and God was the Word:
this was in the beginning with God: all things
were made through him" — in fine, he learned the
teachings of the "prologue" to John's Gospel.
"There also I read that the Word, God, was born
not of flesh, nor of blood, nor of the will of man,
but of God; but that the Word was made flesh,
and dwelt among us, I did not read there." Save
for this omission, Augustine drew from those books,
or read into them, substantially the Christian Gospel — put in other words.

One need not cavil at Augustine's assimilation of
Neoplatonism with the Christianity of the fourth
century. The two had many common sources and
many similarities, — Neoplatonism and its doctrine of the One, the Nous, and the Soul, with
Christianity and its Trinity. Both systems
answered, though with unequal efficacy, to the religious needs of educated men. Over such stepping-
stones thousands had travelled and still were
travelling to Christ. Augustine, by dint of his Neoplatonic studies, won through to the conception of
God as spirit — to the conviction indeed that God

is spirit: πνεῦμα ὁ θεός. The view that evil was
not substance, but privation, also began to dawn
on him. But Neoplatonism lacked the clear and
lovable realisation of the divine, which Christianity
possessed in Christ; and Augustine, like many
others, kept on toward that with his arms out-
stretched.

One of the wonders of the Gospel is that its chief
stumbling-block to thoughtful minds is also the net
by which it captures souls, and holds them fast
when taken: to wit, the Incarnation, — God became Man, the Word became Flesh, and dwelt among
us. It was this that Neoplatonism neither had,
nor could explain or assent to. The thought presented intellectual difficulties almost insurmount-
able. Yet the figure of Christ, his office as Mediator, his saving might as Saviour, drew men with
all the cords of anxiety and hope and dawning love.
To accept him thus, was to cease to be a Neo-
platonist and become a Christian. And this
Christ, when once accepted by the believer's mind,
and taken to his heart, became the fulness of certitude, the blessedness of salvation, the ecstasy of
love. The whole mind and heart of man was
drawn in faith to the divine man Christ, and through
him on to God, realised in Christ as love as well as
power; whom for man to know and love is to be
saved, and in whom is man's delight for ever.

Augustine was led on by the books of the Neoplatonists to think of God as incorporeal, and seek him as the incorporeal truth. Yet they could not bring him the stable enjoyment of this spiritually conceived object of his thought, which should be as well the object of his entire devotion. The strength to rest in the thoughts and love of God, as Augustine knew later, could be had only in and through "the mediator of God and men, the man Christ Jesus." But as yet he thought of Jesus only as a man of excellent wisdom, and could not grasp the mystery of the Word made flesh.

He began to study the Epistles of Paul; and in them he found disclosed the mystery of the law in his members warring against the law of God after the inner man, the flesh lusting against the spirit; and learned that from this conflict, the body of this death, the one deliverance was the grace of God through Jesus Christ. Only through the grace of God in Christ could he reach that peace and stable power of abiding in the love and knowledge and joy of God.

He was now minded to become a Christian, and one day was sharply pricked at hearing the story of the life of St. Anthony. The impulses toward Christ gathering in his soul moved him with power. Their action is set in a dramatic scene in which his bosom's friend Alypius is a silent actor. "What are we about," he cried. "The unlearned storm heaven before us, while we wallow in flesh and blood."

He went out from his house, into the little attached garden, followed by his friend. His mind was in a storm. If he could only end the war between the world's desires and his higher consecration! He broke into tears, and moving away from his wondering friend, cast himself down, weeping, beneath a fig tree. It was not long before a voice was heard saying "take and read"; and remembering that Anthony had been inspired from hearing a Gospel passage, Augustine returned to where he had left the volume of Paul's writings by the side of his friend, opened and read, "not in rioting and drunkenness, not in chambering and wantonness, not in strife and envying; but put ye on the Lord Jesus Christ, and make not provision for the flesh *in concupiscentiis*." He showed the passage to his friend — they knew each other's hearts. Alypius read further: "Him that is weak in faith, receive"; which he applied to his own case. The two entered the house, and told all to Augustine's mother, who exulted and rejoiced. "For Thou didst turn me to Thee, so that I no longer sought for a wife; nor any hope in this world."

Not long after this, Augustine gave up his public professorship, and with his mother and sundry close friends retired to the seclusion of a little villa near Milan. There together they led — he as their master — a life of academic intercourse and devotional meditation. Augustine spent much of his

time inditing philosophic dialogues — the early
writings before alluded to.   The discussions in them,
after the manner of the time, had nothing to do
with exact knowledge, but rather circled round and
round the problems of man's happiness, his immortality, and God's providence.   Such topics en-
grossed the thoughts of spiritually minded pagans
who were seeking "truth," or rather their salvation,
and were inclining toward the assurances of Christianity.

Thus, in "three books," *De Academicis* or *Contra
Academicos*, Augustine takes up the arguments of
those philosophic doubters, and discusses whether
the search for truth, without its attainment, can
make one wise and happy; also what is error, what
is wisdom, what is probable, and what is true; the
opinions of a number of philosophers are considered.
He was composing at the same time his *De beata
Vita*, showing that one cannot be happy when he
has not what he wishes, and that no one is *sapiens*
who is not *beatus*.   With such arguments Augustine
gently pushed himself along toward a Christian
conclusion, that the blessed life consists in the reverent knowledge of the Truth and the full fruition of
it.   At that time he also wrote his *De Ordine*, on
the divine providence; in which a reference to his
praying in tears — illacrymans — shows that the
Christian impulse was moving him emotionally.
As likewise appears in his *Soliloquies*, a book of

devotional reason written at the same time, where, often Platonically, he discusses the two things he desires to know, God and the soul. It may be added that his letters as yet show little that is specifically Christian. On his return to Milan, he wrote upon the immortality of the soul, and afterwards (387–389) composed six books of academic instruction, *De Musica*, chiefly upon versification.

In this country retreat, Augustine had also endeavoured to instruct himself in the Scriptures, by studying Isaiah upon the advice of Ambrose. He was quietly baptised at the Easter celebration in the year 387, his son Adeodatus and his friend Alypius with him. After which it was decided to return to Africa; and the little company journeyed by slow stages to take ship at Ostia, where Monica, his mother, died. It was there that Augustine and his mother, gazing from a window, and discoursing on the things of God, were rapt in an ecstasy of contemplation, to which Christian souls do ever and anon attain, but which as Augustine narrates it, was quite as Neoplatonic as Christian. When his mother was dead, he fell to praying for her soul, as was the custom in the Church.

The stages of Augustine's conversion were affected by his personal equation, and impressed with his individuality. Perhaps they do not reflect directly the general course of conflict with the various phases of paganism, from which Christianity had emerged triumphant. Augustine set forth that conflict, which was also his, more universally in the first ten books of the *City of God*. There, in the name of Christianity, he first refuted the belief that the heathen gods helped their worshippers effectively to the good things of this world, and then the opinion that their power was salutary for the life to come. He also showed that neither fortune nor the position of the stars was the cause of the power of the Roman Empire. Afterwards he took up that most difficult contest of the Faith with the theology of those Greek philosophers who agreed that God existed and had a care for men, yet were not satisfied with worshipping him alone in order to obtain eternal life, but must also practise the cult of many gods besides. They recognised God as above the Soul, the creator of it and of the earth and all things visible; also that the rational principle (to which genus the human soul belongs) is blessed by participation in his unchangeable and incorporeal light. They were called Platonists after the name of Plato.

So Augustine brings Christianity triumphant out from the herd of polytheistic opinions, and finally vindicates its truth in distinction even from the views of Plato (or of Plotinus and Porphyry) who held that beatitude lay not in bodily enjoyment, or even in the enjoyment of mind, but in the enjoyment of God. "Plato calls God the true and highest good, and will have it that the philosopher is a lover of God, and since philosophy makes for the blessed life, the enjoyer of God is that happy one who has loved God " (*Civ. Dei*, viii, 8).

As against views so closely approximating to its highest truths, Augustine could vindicate the Faith only through that Way by which he himself had come, — the name and function and dual nature of Christ. Only through Christ can one come to the true knowledge and the steadfast love and fruition of God. Says Augustine in the *Civitas Dei:* " In qua ut fidentius ambularet ad veritatem, ipsa veritas, Deus Dei filius, homine adsumto, non Deo consumto, eandem constituit et fundavit fidem, ut ad hominis Deum iter esset homini per hominem Deum. Hic est enim mediator Dei et hominum, homo Christus Iesus. Per hoc enim mediator, per quod homo, per hoc et via. Quoniam si inter eum qui tendit et illud quo tendit via media est, spes est perveniendi; si autem desit aut ignoretur qua eundem sit, quid prodest nosse quo eundum sit? Sola est autem adversus omnes errores via munitissima, ut idem sit Deus et homo; quo itur Deus, qua itur homo." [1]

[1] "In order that the mind might advance more confidently toward the truth, the Truth itself, God the Son of God, manhood assumed, deity not destroyed, established and found d this faith, that to man's god there might be a way for man through man god. This is the Mediator of God and men, the man Christ Jesus. For in that he is man he is mediator and also the way. Since if

Thus with final orthodoxy, the Doctor of the Church speaks for the universal Church; for himself he had said that he could not abide with the Platonists because within their doctrines he had not found "illa aedificans caritas a fundamento humilitatis, quod est Christus Jesus" (*Conf.* vii, 20).

In attempting now to indicate the adjustment, the joy and the assurance of salvation which Augustine won, it will not be necessary, nor would it be possible, to explore the broad regions of spiritual development through which his rich nature diffused itself. All writers upon Augustine have found the man and his work, and his suggestiveness, to exceed the compass of their power of formulation — and so did the medieval Church! Even an attempt to outline the manner of his peace is a presumption, so far does the vast testimony of his works exceed the power of our sifting. One may be permitted to note the seemingly indicative points.

Augustine's chief intellectual difficulties had been to conceive the spiritual nature of God, and realise that evil was not substance, but privation or vitiation: "Omnis natura, etiamsi vitiosa est, in quantum natura est, bona est; in quantum vitiosa est, mala

between him who goes and the whither he goes, there leads a way, there is hope of arrival. But if the way is wanting or he does not know how to travel it, what help is there in knowing whither he must go? Now the only way fortified against error is when the same person is at once God and man — God as the goal, man as the way." (*Civ. Dei*, xi, 2).

est" (*Enchiridion*, 13). These difficulties sur-
mounted, then through the lure of Christ he came
to Christ, and through the mediatorship of Christ
he came to God. In the previous course of his life,
he had realised and proved the watchword (so frequently quoted) of his *Confessions:* "fecisti nos ad
te, et inquietum est cor nostrum, donec requiescat in
te." And thenceforth his adjustment, his assurance
of eternal salvation, was to lie, at the end of this un-
quiet course, in the ever fuller and more explicit
realisation of the words of the Psalm which were
always in his heart: "Mihi autem adhaerere deo
bonum est."

God had created us; we had sinned — how?
that is the dark question which Augustine darkly
answers. God by grace and love has redeemed us
through Christ; he has thus restored us to communion with himself. The sin is ours, the grace is
his. The sin is against God, the redemption is
from him altogether, and without him we are helpless, in sin and alienation from our true good, from
the one veritable object of our love and joy.
Through his grace and love we are restored, and
made a new creature, resting in God, — through
Christ. The power of God is perfected in the weakness of human nature. If nearly all of this is Paul,
it is again made new and living with something
added, with something omitted, by which it should
remain the religion of the Western Christian man,

from the fourth century, through the Middle Ages, and through the Reformation.

In the fulfilment of his rôle as defender of the authority of the Church, as vindicator of its sacraments, and as the reinspirer and manifold developer of its doctrine, Augustine at the same time completed his own adjustment, strengthening it in those parts where it was open to attack either by opponents or by his own evolving thought. His exposition of Church doctrine was always a part of his living self, and followed the constructive needs of his searching and desirous genius. The authority of the Church as the efficacious and only channel of grace on earth was attacked by the Donatists; who would also make the efficacy of its officially administered sacraments dependent on the faithfulness of the officiating priest. In combating this sacerdotally untenable position, in maintaining that the Church was the sole authority in matters of faith, and the one door to salvation, Augustine responded to his own need of such an authority, and to the logical requirements of his ecclesiastic nature. For the authority of the Church was a necessary element of his personal peace, which demanded an authoritative interpreter, even guarantor, of the Christian Faith. Had not the authoritativeness of Ambrose held him? And was not the Church verily the entire body of Christ? templum dei, hoc est totius summae trinitatis, sancta est ecclesia, scilicet universa in caelo et in terra (*Enchiridion,* 56). The Church is one; the Church is holy; its union with Christ, its possession of the sanctifying virtue of the Spirit, is not lessened by the sinfulness of any number of individuals belonging to it. It is Catholic, it is Apostolic, it is infallible. Outside of it, and without the virtue of its sacraments, there is no union with God through Christ, there is no redemption, there is no salvation.

Augustine's conceptions of grace and sin were formed before the Pelagian controversy opened; but his convictions fully unrolled themselves only as he defended what was to him of the essence of Christian doctrine and of his own adjustment with God. His faith — the Christian Faith — centres in God's act, that is, in God's grace and love; and not in human virtue, or the building up of character through the action of a virtuously self-directing will; which was the essence of Pelagianism as well as Stoicism. And according to Pelagius's views, human nature, with all its instincts, was essentially capable of good — not essentially corrupted through the inheritance of Adam's sin.

Augustine's human and religious experience had proved for him the falsity of this. He had found his nature corrupt in its concupiscence, and his desires warring against the law of God. Not any virtue of his, not even his own striving, nor any effective energy of his floundering will, but the freely given grace of God through Christ, had annulled his sinfulness and made him a new creature. First came grace, *prevenient* grace, acting in accordance with God's predestinating purpose of salvation for those who are to be called. Its action creates the will to believe — the *velle credere* — in those who are "called according to the purpose"; whereupon with them it becomes coöperating grace. Thus faith is of grace, God's gift. It begins with sheer acceptance, proceeds through trustful obedience, advancing in the perception of God, and works in enlightenment and love. The visible and necessary means of the annulment of original sin and of sins previously committed is the Church's sacrament of baptism. Thereupon the Holy Spirit sheds love in the heart, in place of lust, and the grace of God works itself out in the man's love and corresponding acts, until he realises his justification by faith, and his salvation in the love of God. Through grace and through its sacramental means, man has thus been delivered from a state of sin, in which from lack of God and lack of goodness he could not abstain from sinning further in pride and concupiscence.[1]

Pride and lust are replaced, through Christ, by humility and love. By means of the exemplification of the grace of God in Christ, the human

[1] These last pages are somewhat indebted to Harnack's *History of Dogma.*

Christ primarily, Augustine reaches on to the love and contemplation of God, wherein is man's *summum bonum*, his salvation and eternal life. "Faith, hope and love, and the greatest of these is love;" it is clear that Augustine has worked out this truth of Christ after the manner of Paul: "Nam qui recte amat, procul dubio recte credit et sperat" (*Enchiridion*, 117).

In and through Christ had come the power and assurance of Augustine's love of God, so that he can say, "Not with doubt, but certitude, Lord, I love thee. Thou hast smitten my heart with thy Word, and I have loved thee. But also heaven and earth and all that in them is, lo, from all sides they tell me I should love thee. . . ." "That is the happy life, — beata vita, — to rejoice concerning thee, unto thee, and for thy sake. . . ." "Give me thyself, my God, restore thyself to me. Lo, I love, and if it is little, I would love more. I cannot tell how much my love lacks of what is enough, that my life should run to thy embrace, nor be turned aside, before it is hidden in the hiding place of thy countenance. This much I know, that all is ill with me aside from thee, not only without but within me, and that all my plenty which is not my God, is want." [1] The love of God is the sanction, the proportionment, and the end of the love of all things else. "We

[1] *Conf.* x, 6 and 22; xiii, 8.

T

must love all things with reference to God, otherwise it is lust. Inferior creatures are to be used (*utendum*) with reference to God (*ad Deum*); and our fellows are to be enjoyed (*fruendum*) with reference to God, *toward* God; so thyself; not in thyself ought thou to enjoy (*frui*) thyself, but in him who made thee; thus also shouldst thou enjoy him whom thou lovest as thyself. Therefore let us enjoy ourselves and our brothers in the Lord and not dare to surrender ourselves unto ourselves, downwards as it were." [1]

The Christian *summum bonum* is eternal life. The soul's love of God shall expand in knowledge, and possess the peace of eternal fruition. This is the perfect end, the peace of God, wherein God may be enjoyed and known eternally. In this life, our proper peace is through faith, a pre-fruition of the eternal life which shall be through sight. The peace of earth, — the peace of the body and the soul, the peace of men with each other, lies in concord and the mutual order of obedience — here the great Roman ecclesiastic temper speaks: "the peace of the state is the orderly concord of citizens in commanding and obeying; the peace of the heavenly city is the most ordered and concordant communion in the fruition of God and of each other in God" (*Civ. Dei*, xix, 13).

"God shall be so known to us that he shall be

[1] *De Trinitate*, ix, 13.

seen by the spirit by each of us in ourselves and in each other, and shall be seen in himself, in the new heaven and the new earth and in every creature which shall then exist. . . . And the thoughts within each of us shall be manifest to the others" (*Civ. Dei*, xxii, 29). "What other end is ours — what other peace, what other adjustment, what other salvation — than to come to the kingdom, of which there is no end?" A fitting closing sentence for Augustine's greatest work, and for his life.

CHAPTER XII

THE ARROWS ARE BEYOND THEE

AT the end, what can we think or say of the adjustments of these great men? we pigmies! we little hills to talk of mountains, — of those elemental beings who laid out the paths for humanity to stray in, or, as we hope, move onward; who gave clearest voice to the fears which have oppressed, and the hopes which ever since have lifted men to freedom or to peace. Only a sympathetic and understanding genius, and not the writer of this little book, might haply from the vantage ground of our rising modern decades, place these men, finally analyse their temperaments, their feelings and opinions, fit them into proper categories of partially successful effort, give each his station. Or perchance such a one might so feel the mystery of great personality, his own as well as theirs, that he would make no attempt to determine their positions, their universal values, the possible eternal verities which they expressed.

Yet though we cannot plumb their depths, and proportion their veritable values and relationships, it behooves us, for our own discipline, to order our thoughts concerning them as best we can. This is less to place those somewhat immovable and un-scalable beings, than to range ourselves with respect to them.

At the outset it is easy to settle our minds as to their tangible influence on one another; since we can see where it existed, and where there was none. Between ancient Egypt and Mesopotamia, little mediating influence appears; nor has it been shown with certainty that early currents flowed from Mesopotamia to China. As between China and India, nothing, save certain striking resemblances, points to any interchange of spirit until long after the epoch of Confucius and Lao Tzu, and Gotama, their approximate contemporary. Some centuries elapsed before the Buddha's teachings, considerably expanded and corrupted, became known in China. From India, toward the north and west, no strains of Buddhism or of Brahmanism are found in the religion of Zarathushtra. Nor, until a compara-tively late period, did any Zarathushtrian or Per-sian thought affect the Jews; though the influence of Babylonia upon the children of Abraham is sup-posed to have been from the beginning.

Again, no suggestion from China or India or Persia or Israel stirred the minds of the Greeks, so far as known, before the age of Alexander. After-wards, with the approach of the Christian era, in-fluences fuse together through the Mediterranean world. Hellenism and Judaism affect each other in the way of alien impact and some interpenetration, each carrying to this hostile conjunction whatever quasi-foreign elements it had previously absorbed. Out of Judaism, Christianity arises; and its conquest of the world is in part a shaking off of paganism from its indignant feet, and in part a refashioning of itself to pagan needs.

Turning from the question of traceable influence between them, may we not advantageously proceed from some fundamental human sameness? The impulse of life, of self-fulfilment, was strong in all of them. Each was impelled to seek with the mind, or gain practically through character and temper, the peaceful freedom of thought and mood, or the fearlessness of thought and action, making a suitable adjustment with humanity's needs and limitations — an adjustment which should offer the best fulfilment of the man, the fullest actualisation of his powers and capacities. It may be that the responsive action, the universal fact of responsive action to this common human impulse, represents to our minds a common human validity and truth.

This much at least we may recognise and admit as a universal element, since we find it in ourselves: "The fiend that man harries is [still!] love of the best;" — not the fiend, really, but, as was meant, the god, or human life in its progress. This still drives man on, not to his perdition, but to a more perfect peace, and to a freedom, as he hopes, ever enlarging. Our need of the best, and aspiration to win it, is a living and impelling truth with us, as it was with them. This, whatever else was valid, presents itself to us as the truth running through all the adjustments, the attained freedoms, of these ancient men. This primal verity lies first in the need of the endeavour for the end of happiness and peace. It lies next in the endeavour itself. Who can say but that each great man, even in this endeavour, may have builded better than he knew, have won his good, reached his peace, and gained perhaps the final truth for man? For ourselves, we have found no single answer to life's problem other than life itself, its need-inspired, forward-driving struggle, wherein endeavour is attainment and the path is the goal. And yet with these ancient seers, as with our weakly faltering selves, the tensest fibre of the endeavour which is attainment, is the accompanying vision of a more absolute attainment beyond the sheer endeavour, — the hope for some of them and some of us of a divine and eternal verity of attainment, standing as the cliff upon which the waves of our endeavour beat.

So we think of these men in human generalities, which include both them and us; and next may think of them in generalities which contrast them with ourselves. They, at least, harmonised, even brought to unity, the different factors of their adjustments. Their thinking, and still more evidently their feeling, was a reflex of their experience. Their thought had to do with life, with its ultimate problems. Their intuitions and their reasoned knowledge, working together, kept their convictions whole, kept their lives at one, and themselves wholly possessed of themselves.

This self-possession and unity of life would seem to have sprung from a singleness of spiritual foundation. With Confucius, the Way of Heaven made at once his basic intellectual conception and his supreme devotion. Lao Tzu's and Chuang Tzu's convictions were all involved in their conception of the Tao. The mind and the resolve of Yajnavalkya turn to Brahma, a finished dialectic creation. And with the Buddha, the whole current of his being sets toward his goal of release from suffering, a goal to be attained through dialectic and resolve, and representing a harmony of reason and emotional ardour difficult for us to conceive. The intuitions of the Greek philosophers were likewise in accord with their reason. Every fine concept of Plato's mind was also a desire of his soul, and he brought his desires together in a rejoicing unison within the closure of his concept of God and the idea of the good.

Passing to almost opposite modes of adjustment, we are again convinced that Zarathushtra's devotion to Ahura Mazda corresponded with his reason and the best conceptions of his mind. Likewise, no

need to say that the devotion of the Hebrew prophets
to Yahweh was very part of their expanding thoughts
of Yahweh's righteousness and the compass of his
function in the world.   So Paul, the last Jewish
and first Christian prophet, and so Augustine,
finally, brought his mind's conceptions to accord
with the resistless devotion of his soul.

Whatever the forms of their adjustment, these
men possessed themselves in the accord between
their intellectual convictions and heartfelt devotions,
— one reason why they have proved satisfying to so
many millions.   The long lapse of time, which limits
survivals and sifts the big out of the confusion of
the little, presents them to us as concrete and
definite and simple.   And we are still their children,
we the so-called modern nations of the earth, following, as it were respectively, our great forbears.
How long ago the nations digged the pits in which
they were to lie !   Not so long, of course, if we compare the lapse of previous time, supposedly human,
but long enough when measured by events.   China
is still rooted in the Confucian pit and the morass
of Taoism — nay, perhaps, in these opposite phases
of her temperament.   It were better to speak of
her as standing on the attainment of Confucius
and the considerations of Lao Tzu.   So India might
still stand in contemplation, fixed on her somewhat
slippery Absolute.   If Buddhism has gone forth
from her borders, its spirit still lives in its first home,

while its corrupted or expanded teachings fill so
much of eastern Asia. For us, we likewise are sons
of the Hebrew prophets, and let us hope, the children of Jesus, — even still many of us children of
Paul and Augustine. And are we not as well the
sons of the Greeks ?

These men have passed on —

"Leaving great verse unto a little clan."

Yet they were as the mustard seed, which should
become a mighty tree, with generations upon generations of fowls lodging in its branches. Did they
not excel in deep enthusiastic well-being ? reaching
their various adjustments with such assurance that
acquiescence on their part became cordial acceptance, even a passionate acceptance of what life, or
the universal ways, held for them, or God lovingly
bestowed ?

Modern thought has expanded the manifold of
life's mysteriousness. Perceiving its exhaustless
mysteries at so many more points than pricked
these ancients, men no longer can attain to such
clean and concrete adjustments, with such well-
hemmed edges. Which may be quite as it should
be, in the broadening ways of human progress.

Before trying at last to fit our categories of discrimination to those men, we recall how thoughtful
were their adjustments, even those which rested
directly on heroic mood. It may also be said that

with none of them did the main feature of his scheme of life exclude other factors of assurance. With the most self-reliant, there is some looking to a power not themselves, perhaps for aid, at all events with a respectful taking of that power into account. While those who throw themselves on God, like Paul or Augustine, know that their own efforts also are needed to maintain a conduct according with their faith. "Not I, but the grace of God, — not I, but the spirit of Christ within me," — however whole-souledly Paul or Augustine might trust in God, and accept his spirit to the dispossession and replacement of their former selves, each knew the strenuousness of the endeavour required even to keep himself a cleanly vessel of God's grace.

Again disclaiming the ability to place these men according to their actual and lasting values, we must try to distinguish, and order our own thinking in regard to them. We must perforce use categories sounding in our own conceptions of the kinds of life which men may lead with serious approval. If those ancients would not have recognised our categories, as applied to them, they, nevertheless, have been the source from which our constructive thoughts largely have been taken.

Asia — the East — inclines to vagueness, and also holds less firmly or less passionately than the West to human personality, and to the demands and full development of the individual.   Confucius was a tremendous person — Chinese tradition does not err in making him nine feet high. He was a very great social and political organiser. He would set his people, as he had fixed himself, within a beneficent web of rites and ceremonies, formative of character, constructive and preservative of the State. It was a scheme following the Way of Heaven, to which men must conform with unremitting care. This made Confucius's adjustment. While the detail was a meticulous web, the unifying principle, the norm of human life, was vague and impersonal. It could utter no commands, but could only exemplify itself and its ways as the standard of conduct. Lao Tzu, Chuang Tzu, also looking to the Way, found therein quite other exemplification — found therein the opposite of any mandate of action, and no inducement to painstaking and minute observance. Contemplation of the Tao — the Eternal Way, the All, the Absolute, the What-not — in its endless construction and undoing, was their adjustment. Their contemplative acquiescence conformed to the *laisser-aller* of the Absolute; and naturally with no obstinate retention of the individuality of each temporary acquiescing human form. As inaction is vaguer than action, so Taoism is vaguer, even in its principles, than Confucianism.

In India the human adjustment is not merely careless of the individual; it has ensconced itself in detestation of concrete, pestilentially changing, individuality : its end, its attainment, lies in the final elimination of that. So with Brahmanism in its affirmation of the Absolute; so with Buddhism in its denial of the same.

A change indeed to reach the land of Zarathushtra, the fighting ally of his righteous warring God. No acquiescence here, no negative adjustment; but victory over evil foes, and the reward of life thereafter. Ahura is somewhat less clearly conceived than Yahweh — who also "teacheth my hands to war and my fingers to fight." Of all celestial characters, Yahweh is drawn with most trenchant line — a tremendous *dramatis persona*. If we have not seen his form, we have heard his voice, and through unmistakable utterances have been taught his will, and with what blows from his rod have been driven to do it ! — his rod of punishment, his rod of love, his rod of promise ! Yahweh was an individual ! a personality ! In obeying him, in following his ways, the Jew developed his individuality, or, if one will, the individuality of that most individual race.

The Greek gods possessed a full store of human waywardness. They are revealed through poetry. The Greek did not develop his character from conscious obedience to them; but quite consciously out of his own strength and reason, and out of the sword-play and compromise of the energies of his desires. Nor did the Roman draw motives of development from his gods; rather, before as well as after he had eaten of the Greek tree of knowledge, he evolved himself by virtue of his own tenacity.

Christianity — Jesus, Paul, Augustine. Were they not of the heritage of Israel? and Augustine, perhaps Paul, of the heritage of Greece and Rome as well? It may be that from Christianity came the final building up of individuality for the ancient world. Assuredly there came from it, both for that world and our own, the final adjustment of the individual with God's power and love, in which he, the individual Christian, was saved and completed and fulfilled. He who giveth his life, shall save and redeem and fulfil himself: bread thrown upon the waters, returning after many days as the new bread of life. The characters of Christians differed; in various ways they gained the peace and profitable freedom of their great adjustment, through grace freeing their spirits in the truth that maketh free, and in perfect accord with almighty power, fulfilling their lives to all eternity in the love of God.

Each of these marked adjustments of the ancient world held elements belonging to the rest. One may observe that in their sequence and succession they tend to change and merge into each other. Their protagonists, ranged according to the attitude of each toward his individual destiny, will fall into two loose-bordered groups: contemplators, and those moved by a closer personal purpose. The contemplator appears to stand outside his destiny,

and to contemplate it or something else. In the
other group, the man and his happiness, his peace
and freedom, are incorporate in his destiny, hang
upon it : he moves and has his being in the thought
of his fortunes upon earth or his lot thereafter.

In some way, the Contemplators find their peace
and freedom in considering the Universe, or in
meditating upon their natures and the connection
between their destinies and the universal order.
They may think or dream themselves around and
above the processes of nature and necessity. Thus
they become the equal or superior of what they cannot resist, by realising its infinitude : "L'homme n'est
qu'un roseau, le plus faible de la nature, mais c'est un
roseau pensant ! " Lao Tzu is here, and his disciple
Chuang Tzu. They realise the universe, and their
own natures as held within its all-embracing ways.
They love its infinite range, and bathe in the amplitude
of the mystery of life. Potent dreamers they, who
could dream far out beyond the reach of their individual lot, which they held as lightly as it held them.

The Brahmans of India did not dream as suavely,
nor with equal imagination ; but they reasoned with
insistent metaphysical acuteness. They did not so
serenely rest above their personal destinies.
Chuang Tzu, knowing that his being would be
scattered to its elements, smiled at the prospect.
The Brahmans were pricked by the need to think
out their release. Their thought was not sheer

contemplation, but was goaded by longing for freedom from desire, and for freedom from the tormenting impermanence of individuality. As for Gotama, the Buddha, the motive of his arduous thinking appears the same. But the desire to point out to others the path to salvation lifted his personal adjustment to Saviourhood, and made him the revealer of a universal refuge; in other words, the founder of a religion.

From the East to the West, the temper changes, and contemplators may be called more fitly investigators. The Greek *vita contemplativa* becomes a happy devotion to the quest of knowledge. At first the philosophers are busier investigating the world about them than in considering their place in it, or their inner nature and particular destiny. But, in time, the processes of thought and contemplation come homing back to the thinker. Thereupon the western tenacity of individuality impresses itself on the intellectual energy which is occupied with investigation, and the thinker can no longer stand aloof from interest in his present welfare and future destiny. The line of early Greek thinkers passes on to Democritus, to Socrates, to Plato; and the search for truth is impressed forever with eudaimonism, that is to say, with the compelling sense of the determining significance and importance of the welfare and happiness of the individual thinker. It was Plato who enriched the contem-

plative adjustment with that blessed mood arising
from beautiful conceptions realised as part of the
soul of man and its perfecting. Then through the
belief, uplifted and glorified by him, of the immortality of the ennobled soul, he made absolute the
central value of the individual man and his destiny.
This was his crowning contribution to spiritual freedom. After him, Aristotle gathered all knowledge
as the basis and content of his intellectual satisfaction. With less temperamental geniality and
colder mentality than Plato, he fixed the apex of his
happiness in the contemplation of unmoved but all-
moving causes.

So Plato linked the contemplative adjustment to
the blessedness of the immortal soul. His golden
joinder of intellectuality and hope looked with a
lover's eyes to God — such lover's eyes becoming
rather steely gray with Aristotle. Succeeding to the
Aristotelian universality of intellectual interest,
philosophy, in Stoicism, ceased to be worthy of the
name, so narrowly did it restrict its considerations
to that which made for man's peace of mind. Stoicism began as an adjustment of the self-reliant soul,
even as did Epicureanism. In the course of years,
the self-reliance staled; Epicureanism had nothing
to turn to, while Stoicism, through its more energetic conception of the Divine, became prayerful —
the Stoic began to look beyond himself for the
complete assurance of his peace.

U

Thus the *vita contemplativa*, having centred its interest in the contemplator's welfare and destiny, found that it could not insure the one or fulfil the other. Incidentally the self-reliant intellect has proved itself limited, terrestrial, and unable to satisfy a nature which is conscious of having to do with eternity. As a means of human adjustment and deliverance, philosophic thought has broken down. For aid and comfort, for peace and assurance, for blessedness, in fine, the thinker turns to God. The freedom and assurance of his life have assumed the mode and form of salvation.

Clearly we have passed from the group who stand above their destinies, content to contemplate the universe, and themselves as elements of its resistless processes. We are in the company of those whose adjustment with life is vitally incorporate in the destiny of their individual selves. Moreover, we have become, let us hope fruitfully, entangled with another principle in the ordering of our adjustments. Those men who stood above their destinies, in disinterested contemplation of the universe, or content with the quest of knowledge, were utterly self-reliant, even unconsciously so: for the height of self-reliance is to be unconscious of relying on oneself and not upon another. As the former group of adjustments pass into those which are insistent on the welfare of the protagonist, they pass through a stage of self-reliance which has become self-conscious; and then into the stage where conscious self-reliance gives way to a conscious lack of it, and at last becomes a yearning for divine salvation.

Hereupon, however, a complementary and final element enters; the love of that Power upon which the man relies to safeguard and complete his destiny. This may become absorbing devotion, an energy which carries the man again beyond himself, and once more may lift him above personal anxiety. In the great exemplars of this devotion — indeed in the Great Exemplar — trust in God, communion with Him, is perfect; while solicitude as to salvation is lost in consecration to God's saving purposes. In this way, the obedient and co-operating zeal of the Servant in Isaiah is completed in the sonship of Jesus: "Surely Yahweh will do nothing, but he reveals his secret to his servants the prophets." With more absolute union, "the Father loveth the Son, and hath given all things into his hand," and "the Son can do nothing of himself, but what he seeth the Father doing."

In Paul, the need of salvation has become again a driving energy, while devotion to the salvation of his fellows, his working unison with the grace of God, likewise consumes him. He symbolises the varying moods of Christians after him, whose need of salvation is compelling. Augustine is in this category. With Paul and Augustine, however, and countless other Christians, the sense of God and of the Saviour's deed and constant function, leads to a grateful surrender of the saved one to Him who has saved him — a surrender offered in confidence and love, if not in self-abandonment.

Who shall say whether the pendulum might not thus swing back to an abandonment of human individuality ? The course taken by the development of personality in Western Asia and Eastern Europe had led to the need which only Christianity satisfied. The need was a religious need; a religious adjustment was required. Through the near preceding centuries, the human personality had become acutely conscious of itself, and of its cardinal importance. It had also arrived at the realisation that it could not save and fulfil itself, and of itself attain its rightful destiny. Christianity offered this salvation and fulfilment, offered them through the agency of divine and human personality, that of God the Father and Christ. The Gospel was a reaching out of the fulness of divine personality to the need of human personality, — and not only a reaching out in power but an intimate bestowal of comfort, with love close and personal. Such a divine giving safeguarded and assured the recipient in the eternal love and power of God. His most unqualified surrender of himself could be only unto such safekeeping. The conception of salvation is thus completed in the answer of the human love to the divine; the Christian fulfils himself in the love of God. Herein, as

a religious adjustment, Christianity would seem
final.

Another question of import as to the Gospel's
finality was to arise from the intellectual and inquisitive side of human nature, and keep itself insistent.   How did the Gospel bear upon the growth
and expansion of the human mind through knowledge ?   Was it antagonistic or favourable ? relevant
or irrelevant ?   The varying answers which have
been given to this question, or have somehow been
lived out, extend through the centuries called by the
Christian name.   The age which first received the
Gospel did not care supremely for knowledge.   When
Augustine declared that he would know God and
the soul, and these alone, he uttered the intensest
cravings of his nature, which were not for knowledge.
With other men in other times, God and the soul
might include the universe of God-created things.

In its acceptance, or in its application to life, the
Gospel could be narrowed or broadened.   It was
adapted to the humblest human want, and yet
sufficient for the soul uplifted to its heights of love
and spiritual consecration.   It did not speak directly
to the inquisitive mind, not being a method of intellectual living.   But the mind of man, — the full
compass of his intellectual cravings and faculties,
— is from God.   If the Gospel was salvation, was
it not to be salvation for the whole man ?   Could
it not "save" the uttermost reaches of his mind,

as well as the purest impulses of his love? How should it hamper the humanity which it had come to save eternally?

And still the human personality gives one pause. It seems so necessarily a passing phase, not to be imagined as lasting forever, or as the vehicle of an eternal here and now. Think of eternity and of thyself, O man! Do the two fit each other? The body is impermanent. The mind also unfolds with the human years, changing and finite. Whether embodied or disembodied, is it suited for eternity? Would it think its thoughts, or love its loves, forever? Must not its finitude tire? Could it love even God, and think on Him and the universe, eternally? The last is perhaps the most tolerable idea that can be linked with an enduring finite personality. Yet Christian rapture has tended to pass on, *through* this conception, as it were; has sought to lose itself in God, to become in and of Him. Musing saints have anticipated deliverance from themselves. Only absorption in Deity contents them. Through His eyes only would they see; only through His heart would they love. Less rapturous, more analytic, tempers also may conclude that only infinite life is suited to eternity: not man, but God.

THE following pages contain advertisements of Macmillan books by the same author.

The Classical Heritage of the Middle Ages

By HENRY OSBORN TAYLOR

Cloth, 12mo, 402 pages, $1.75 net; postage extra

THIRD EDITION

The subject of this book is the transition from the Classical to the Mediaeval. It follows the changes undergone by classic thought, letters, and art, on their way to form part of the intellectual development of the Middle Ages, and shows how pagan tastes and ideals gave place to the ideals of Christianity and to Christian sentiments. The argument reaches backward to classic Greece and Rome and forward into the Middle Ages; but the discussion centres in the period extending from the fourth to the seventh century. This period was strikingly transitional in Italy and the western provinces of the Roman Empire; before it had passed, the various elements of classic culture had assumed the forms in which they were to make part of the intellectual life of the Middle Ages, and Christianity had taken on a mediaeval character.

CONTENTS

THE MACMILLAN COMPANY
Publishers   64-66 Fifth Avenue   New York